EXPLORING 3D

THE NEW GRAMMAR OF STEREOSCOPIC FILMMAKING

EXPLORING 3D
THE NEW GRAMMAR OF STEREOSCOPIC FILMMAKING

ADRIAN PENNINGTON

CAROLYN GIARDINA

Focal Press
Taylor & Francis Group

NEW YORK AND LONDON

First published 2013
by Focal Press
70 Blanchard Road, Suite 402, Burlington, MA 01803

Simultaneously published in the UK
by Focal Press
2 Park Square, Milton Park, Abingdon, Oxon OX14 4RN

Focal Press is an imprint of the Taylor & Francis Group, an informa business

Notices
Knowledge and best practice in this field are constantly changing. As new research and experience broaden our understanding, changes in research methods, professional practices, or medical treatment may become necessary.

Practitioners and researchers must always rely on their own experience and knowledge in evaluating and using any information, methods, compounds, or experiments described herein. In using such information or methods they should be mindful of their own safety and the safety of others, including parties for whom they have a professional responsibility.

Product or corporate names may be trademarks or registered trademarks, and are used only for identification and explanation without intent to infringe.

Library of Congress Cataloging in Publication Data
CIP data has been applied for

ISBN: 978-0-240-82372-0 (pbk)
ISBN: 978-0-240-82386-7 (ebk)

Typeset in Univers-Light
by TNQ Books and Journals, Chennai, India

Contents

FOREWORD

Courtesy of DreamWorks Animation.

n life, there are AHA! moments, which provide sudden clarity about an issue. And then
here are OMG! moments, which are AHA! moments multiplied by 100. These are the
mes when you must accept that your world is about to change forever.

experienced an OMG! moment on November 28, 2004. That was when I visited
n IMAX theater to see the film *The Polar Express* in digital 3D. [NOTE: The movie
pened on 11/14/04 … maybe your calendar shows the date you actually saw it.] I was
pellbound. The images were crisp and clear, the sense of depth was startling and, most
emarkably, the 3D dramatically immersed me and the rest of the audience in the story.
he wall of the screen had dissolved into an open window, drawing us into the film while
lso releasing the characters into the theater. It was almost as if we were viewing a
ompletely different movie from the 2D version that was playing across the country.

Vell, on that OMG! day, *The Polar Express* may have held me spellbound, but it also
ave me a stomach ache. I felt I had seen the future, and realized that our studio would

need to race into that future as quickly as possible. This would require a complete retooling of our operations. The following day, I convened an urgent meeting of our senior staff. We set a course that would lead to DreamWorks Animation becoming the world's first studio to make and release 100% of its films in 3D.

Now, Adrian Pennington and Carolyn Giardina have written this fascinating and authoritative book to explain the future to us. In it, they detail everything you need to know about this amazing new technology: what goes into the making of a digital 3D film, how it is used to enrich the storytelling experience, and why this is the most important development for the movie business in more than seven decades. Long ago, our industry experienced two other technological revolutions. The first was synchronized sound in 1927, and the second was the three-strip Technicolor process in 1935. Since then, there have certainly been meaningful enhancements, such as widescreen projection and stereo sound. But it wasn't until the arrival of digital 3D that we have seen another fundamental transformation of the medium.

At DreamWorks Animation, it has been extraordinary to be making films at this amazing time in Hollywood history. With each new movie we produce, 3D is taking us to fantastic new places in visual storytelling. Indeed, we can relate to the sense of discovery that filmmakers must have felt back in the '20s and '30s, when sound and color were added to their creative toolbox.

And there is no question that we are just at the beginning of this revolution. Master directors like Martin Scorsese, Steven Spielberg, and James Cameron are pushing 3D in innovative new directions. Looking ahead, the cost barriers to this technology will be coming down, making it increasingly available to filmmakers at every budget level. So, we can expect the impact of stereoscopic motion pictures to continue to build and won't be fully felt for years to come.

In the meantime, we have this book to serve as a roadmap to the revolution. For anyone interested in the history, the craft and, yes, the magic of movies, this is essential reading. It is full of countless AHA!s, as it tells how 3D is changing the world of cinema.

In short, OMG!

ACKNOWLEDGEMENTS

The authors would like to thank all of those who were interviewed for this book—for their time, expertise, and enthusiasm.

We would especially like to thank Jeffrey Katzenberg for contributing the foreword and DreamWorks Animation for use of their image on the cover.

Thank you also to the companies that provided images that appear in this book, including 3net; All England Lawn Tennis Club; Atlantic Productions; Bazmark; Cameron|Pace Group; Cirque du Soleil; Creative Differences Productions; DreamWorks Animation; Electric Sky Productions; GK Films; HBS; LAIKA; Neue Road Movies; Oxford Scientific Films; Paramount Pictures; RealD and the ROH; Sony Europe and Sony Pictures.

The authors also wish to thank everyone who assisted us with introductions, arranging interviews, background information, and securing photographs, especially:

Jeff Hare, David Hail, Monica Dejbakhsh and Anne Globe at DreamWorks Animation; Jerry Schmitz; Maggie Begley and LAIKA; Monique Villareal; Dorothea Sargent; Jason Armitage; Ann Boyd; Rod Riegel; Nicola Taylor and the HBS production team; Grae Hillary; Louise Bryce; Mervyn Hall, Thomas Lovelock; Reinhard Penzel; Tim Clutton-Brock; Heidi Frankl at Neue Road Movies; Charlie Coombes; Cynthia Shapiro; Lise Dubois and Renée-Claude Menard; Steve Schklair; Catherine Owens; Simon Sieverts; Phil Streather; Julian Napier; Kim Lavery; Dave Gouge at Weta Digital; Laura Barber; Colin Ritchie; Leah James and Rachael Fung at Bazmark; Anton Monsted; Barrie M. Osborne; Stephen Rivkin A.C.E.; Lisa Frechette, Lea Yardum, and Michelle Benson.

We would also like to thank Fergal Ringrose at *TVBEurope,* and Owen Phillips and Gregg Kilday at *The Hollywood Reporter.*

Many thanks to Dennis McGonagle for spotting the project's potential and for walking us through the process and Carlin Reagan our editor at Focal Press.

1

THE NEW GRAMMAR OF STEREOSCOPIC FILMMAKING

Following the recent wave of stereoscopic 3D film and TV content there is a growing body of opinion that if 3D is ever to be more than a theme park experience the potential of the new format needs far greater artistic exploration.

There is a need, not just for technically accurate stereo 3D to create a comfortable viewing experience, but for a creatively enhancing 3D that lifts content away from novelty and mundanity and into the art form of filmmaking.

Curious directors are beginning to see the potential of stereo 3D as a visual storytelling tool and to embed it into productions from inception as one would use lighting or sound.

Such filmmakers have instinctively reached for artistic metaphors with which to describe the new medium at their disposal. Working on *Hugo*, Academy Award winner Martin Scorsese likened the technology to cubism and sculpture, understanding that characters and objects can be seen from new perspectives and need no longer be fixed to a flat canvas. "Picasso and Braque went to see films between 1909 and 1912 and were fascinated by the idea that on a flat screen you could see different aspects of the same figure because they move," says Scorsese. "This seemed to translate into cubism."

Perhaps, he suggests, 3D cinema can provide the illusion of seeing around people and objects. "With sculpture you walk around it so it becomes something different every place you look. In doing so you are visually performing a tracking shot. Suddenly the sculpture has a very powerful presence with different aspects to it and that is the effect that 3D delivers."

He also sees parallels in dance. "When you see dancers move on stage, the depth between their bodies allows you to see a fluid sense of the visual field they are moving in. The only thing that approximates that in 2D cinema is camera movement. Add to that the illusion of depth and you have something that is not simply a flat image but something that opens up to infinite possibility. It is no longer cinema that we know."

Director Wim Wenders (*Paris, Texas; The Buena Vista Social Club*) has also compared 3D direction to sculpture. Struggling to find a way to capture the choreography of Pina Bausch on film, he claims, "It was only when 3D was added to the language of film that I could enter dance's realm. 3D, with its illusion of depth, could open out the flatness of the cinema screen and give dance the depth and sculptural quality it needed to work cinematically."

Some of the most successful Hollywood producers, once dubious of the new medium, are converts. Baz Luhrmann needed to convince Barrie M. Osborne, the Oscar-winning producer of *The Lord of the Rings* trilogy, that his proposed literary adaptation of *The*

"I was a skeptic who thought 3D was a fad," admits *Gatsby*'s Executive Producer. "However having gone through the experience I would definitely consider 3D for future projects. The use of 3D to compose a shot and story can make a scene much more powerful. The power of the actor's performance and personalities is heightened."

Given that Peter Jackson has shot *The Hobbit* in 3D, Osborne unsurprisingly suggests that "were the technology as advanced then as it is now, I think we would have made *The Lord of the Rings* in 3D."

For *Avatar* producer and Oscar winner Jon Landau, stereo 3D can create an "almost voyeuristic experience" as well as a "sensory experience."

He says, "In the past, for the most part, 3D had been relegated to the B movies—it wasn't for new, original studio tentpole pictures. I think *Avatar* showed audiences that 3D doesn't have to be a gimmick, that it can be a core part of the filmmaking process and the theater-going experience."

Stereoscopic 3D is not new of course. It has been around since the very foundations of filmmaking and there have been several books and many articles written about the history of previous incarnations. The current vogue has come about because all the technical elements from digital cinematography cameras to mass market display on cinema and TV screens have made it practicable.

For Landau the backdrop of the wider transition to digital production is more significant than the arrival of 3D alone. "There are many filmmakers and cinematographers who have spent careers working in [35mm] film and for whom the biggest change is not the ability to shoot 3D but to shoot digitally," he says.

While critics continue to contend that 3D will be a passing fad, or at best a niche suitable only for select blockbusters, others believe that this time around stereoscopy will grow to become as ubiquitous as two-dimensional imagery is today. Indeed there are some who believe that for the past 100 years or more cinema has been missing a trick.

Some of the earliest stills photography deployed stereo processing as a matter of course. Stereoscopic stills from the 1860s have, for example, been used as the basis of a four-hour documentary series about the American Civil War, featured here in a section examining how 3D has impacted the documentary genre.

At the very birth of cinema its founding fathers Georges Méliès and the Lumière brothers dabbled in stereoscopic short films with the Lumière brothers reshooting their original *L'Arrivée d'un Train* (1896) in 1935 stating that stereo was how they had conceived cinema would evolve. In *Hugo*, his astute evocation of the period, rendered in 3D and featuring reconstructions of *L'Arrivée d'un Train* and the fantasy films of Méliès, Scorsese underscores their vision.

"Once the moving image arrived people wanted sound, colour and depth but depth has always been experimental—because of the technology and cost," says Scorsese. "Méliès would have gone there, and did, since two minutes of film he shot in stereo has survived."

Stereo 3D may trick our mind into believing that the images we see are three-dimensional but proponents of the format argue that since we see in three dimensions 3D is simply a more realistic, more natural approximation for how we experience life. Similarly, just as we hear sound surrounding us, so audio technology has evolved from mono to stereo to surround sound to help us support our belief in what we are seeing on screen.

"Our physiological ability to negotiate the world through spatial awareness works very well between distances of 50 cm to about 10 meters," notes Jamie Beard, Previs Supervisor at Weta Digital. "I can only theorize that we need this information about our immediate surroundings in order for us to move about. It is no coincidence that stereo 3D is best at this range also—it reflects the same responses we have to the real world."

"For instance, 3D works particularly well when we look down almost as if we respond more to dimensionality when it feeds our fear of falling."

Stereo 3D comes closer to simulating human vision, but can only approximate our depth perception. Unlike other art forms which are created in space—notably sculpture and theater—we cannot physically move our heads or bodies in stereo 3D to see around an object. Filmmakers must direct the way we perceive depth just as they are directing our view of a subject and of a scene by composition and focus.

"To me, 3D is a tool that allows you to visualize a scene in a way that you would if you could be there to see it yourself," says Joe Letteri, a four-time Academy Award-winning visual effects supervisor (including one for *Avatar*) and partner in digital effects facility Weta Digital. "That is its biggest strength and biggest promise."

"Once you have the idea as a basis, you can work with that as a creative tool, for example to get the audience to focus on certain parts of the frame to enable the storytelling."

This philosophy informed the 3D choices in *Avatar*. "The primary goal was to give you a sense of presence and being there," explains Letteri. "And on top of that to work in specific cues for the audience to be able to follow the action, guiding them to where they should be looking within a frame and across shots.

"If viewers are fishing around the screen not knowing where to look, it becomes uncomfortable. If they have to do it too much, the experience starts to fall apart."

Cinematographers represent depth using a variety of techniques that have become ingrained in our understanding of what it means to watch a motion picture. Techniques such as perspective, selective focus (depth of field), movement, framing, variations in scene brightness, and other depth cues like shadow and texture can convey the depth of a scene. This entrenched cinematic grammar must obey the physical constraints of the size, shape, and position of the screen plane itself. Stereo 3D however promises a broader palette.

Fig. 1.1 *How to Train Your Dragon* used 3D to underscore the film's emotional connection.
"How To Train Your Dragon" © 2010, Courtesy of DreamWorks Animation.

"We have to deal with an art that has established itself over a century, with an incredibly intricate and elaborate grammar and vocabulary that we love and cherish, but we which we should perhaps see as some sort of a mistake—a two-dimensional film with the second eye missing," Wenders argues.

According to Wenders, 3D belongs in the hands of "people willing and able to forget limits, rules, formulas, recipes, and enter a whole new age of cinema, where there is more…connection. Existential connection. Believe it or not, 3D has that connecting power."

He goes further and suggests that stereo 3D could move beyond mere imitation of real life, transcending it perhaps.

"These stories will need some sort of affinity to space, to depth and to volume," Wenders says. "I can't help thinking that the next groundbreaking film needs to be an intimate piece, maybe a simple story trying to transcend everyday life. A film that is thriving on moods, on existential situations, on a description of contemporary living."

Phil "Captain 3D" McNally, Global Stereoscopic Supervisor, DreamWorks Animation

Courtesy DreamWorks Animation

"You can think of stereo as a dial on the palette of filmmaking tools that you can increase or decrease with the emotional intensity of the story.

In its simplest form, the benefit of stereoscopic depth over a traditional 2D movie is if you want to be closer to the character, you can really make the character closer. Whether that's a pleasant closeness—because the character is attractive—or whether it is unpleasant—because the characters is for instance an evil dictator—the fact that you can use the space in front of the screen to literally invade your personal space as a viewer is a very powerful tool. Also, if you want to feel remote from someone, you can push them back to make them feel far away and make them very distant. We adjust the stereo from shot to shot—and even within a shot—to heighten intensity.

I would encourage people to stop thinking about this as making a 3D movie—that can put you in the gimmick/cliché mode—and start thinking about making a spatial movie. When you start thinking about spatial moviemaking that puts you in a different mindset that is more positive for stereoscopic filmmaking. Spatially, what do you want this scene to do or what can this scene add to the story?"

A Creative Discipline

Through the words of filmmakers, we'll examine the potential of 3D to better tell a story through adding elements and features that 2D can never achieve.

Getting there means shifting the focus from thinking about 3D as a purely technical discipline or a cost issue toward a vocabulary that concentrates on the potential of stereo to enhance mood and emotion or help convey a feeling of connection with an actor's performance, a landscape, or a narrative.

"With each new movie we produce, 3D is taking us to fantastic new places in visual storytelling," declares DreamWorks Animation CEO Jeffrey Katzenberg. "And there is no question that we are just at the beginning of this revolution."

Those interviewed for this book believe passionately that 3D is a creative discipline and that only a creative approach will determine whether stereo 3D will this time stay for good.

Of course there is a precedent for 3D mainly attracting technical-minded enthusiasts. "From the 1950s until now, 3D has attracted a lot of technical people," says Stereo Supervisor Phil "Captain 3D" McNally, whose credits include DreamWorks Animation's *How to Train Your Dragon* and *Puss In Boots*, and Disney's *Chicken Little* and *Meet the Robinsons*. "There was certainly an association with stereo that it was a technical not a creative thing, which I think is completely wrong," he says.

"If you listed the components of what make up a shot— framing, lighting, lens choice, staging—stereo is just one of those things on the list," he continues. "You've got to think of it in balance with every other component compositionally. And of course what is driving your decision is, 'What is the point of the story that requires this shot?'"

Adds McNally: "The difficulty with stereo in that mix is that everyone has great experience with all of the other components and very little experience with the stereo component. In that sense it needs some positive discrimination. There is emphasis being put on the weakest link while people get educated."

Digital 3D has had an uneven start. There have been highlights in both animation and live action productions, but there have also been many uses of the medium that have been considered mediocre at best.

"Some very big blockbuster films are clear indications that everyone wanted to ride the 3D wave but had no intention of telling the story in 3D," contends Buzz Hays, senior

Fig. 1.2 3D comes closer to simulating human vision, but can only approximate our depth perception.

PINA, Thusnelda and Dominique Mercy and Clémentine Deluy © NEUE ROAD MOVIES, photograph by Donata Wenders.

vp, 3D production, Sony Pictures Technologies. "For the time being a 3D version of a 2D story is a way into 3D for studios and directors but their attempts do not push the medium forward."

Looking back, many new filmmaking techniques have seen such periods of development, experimentation, and finessing before they became accepted.

It took time to perfect the mechanics of chemically developing a color negative, and even more time for filmmakers to bring color theory to their filmed stories, lending it creative credibility.

"Right now people are stuck trying to solve technical problems and the question of the creative use of 3D has been a secondary concern," says 3D supervisor Rob Engle. He has amassed credits on a string of stereoscopic features, including *The Polar Express*, *Monster House*, *Beowulf*, *Pirates of the Caribbean: On Stranger Tides*, and *The Amazing*

Spider-Man. "If all you do is think about 2D filmmaking techniques then you won't get something that is nearly as satisfying as if you really involve 3D in a project from beginning to end."

He believes stereo adds a layer of intensity to the photography that you don't get in 2D. "Successful filmmakers are beginning to recognize that the power of 3D in not in the gimmickry, but in the ability to connect with audiences in ways that are harder to do in 2D," Engle says.

Fig. 1.3 Library of Congress, Prints & Photographs Division, Civil War Photographs.

Fig. 1.4 Stereo stills photography was a popular art form from the 1860s onwards and only waned with the arrival of moving pictures at the turn of the century. 3net's *Fields of Valor: The Civil War* mixes stereo 3D reenactments with stereo photographs from the period.

Library of Congress, Prints & Photographs Division, Civil War Photographs.

Vince Pace who co-developed, with James Cameron, the camera systems used to shoot *Avatar*, advises filmmakers not to abandon their learned storytelling skills.

"(3D) is one of many different tools that a filmmaker will use to create entertainment," Pace says. "Too often filmmakers come to 3D thinking they have to concentrate on the 3D element when many of the fundamental skills that are needed to create a piece of filmed storytelling are already established in 2D. Filmmakers do not have to leave everything they have learnt behind and start to learn a new language."

As more and more work is done and as filmmakers move onto their second or third 3D projects, lessons are being learned and guidelines laid down about what it takes to produce good 3D. More often than not though "good" 3D refers to the technicalities of ensuring there are no edge violations or great leaps in convergence and divergence that a viewer's eyes are asked to make between cuts.

Guidelines are there to guide. Even UK broadcaster Sky, which sets strict benchmarks for the standard and consistency of programs destined for its 3D channel, would be the first to admit that its guidelines are not rules. It encourages exploration of stereoscopy provided the basics have been digested. What makes "good" creative use of 3D is therefore up for grabs.

Technology continues to evolve at a breakneck pace. Regularly it seems there is enhancement to the resolution of a camera's sensor or new software to automate parts of the workflow. Any print article trapping technology at a certain point in time will quickly pass its consume-by date. Yet the ideas and approaches to using spatial information in film and the creative thinking behind certain decisions to create a 3D effect are just being born and will have a longer lifespan.

Few people, for example, refer to the type of camera, specific crane, or exact film negative that Orson Welles employed on *Citizen Kane* but his film is still used as a textbook for how to craft scenes 70 years on—scenes that are full of invention and built, according to the young director himself (of RKO Studios) with "the biggest electric train set a boy ever had."

In any case, the technology has matured. "In 2008 3D broadcasting was all about whether we could actually transmit any pictures. By 2010 it was about building a technical production stream and by 2011 we had a fully functioning workflow," says Duncan Humphreys, Creative and Technical Director at CAN Communicate, a partner in the production of the live 3D broadcast of the 2010 FIFA World Cup. "The technology is proven. While there will continue to be technological developments, from here on in the focus is on refining the editorial."

Chris Parks, Stereographer, *Jack the Giant Killer*

Image courtesy Chris Parks.

"3D isn't about objects but about the space between objects. When composing a scene, don't think about it in terms of foreground, middle ground, and background, but in terms of the air that is contained, or the volumes that the objects define. That way you will create satisfying, interesting, and involving scenes that will feel well-rounded and continuous, rather than separate elements.

This creative approach will determine whether 3D will have longevity as a product. The audience comes to the cinema with decades of 2D film grammar lodged in their brain but there's a new film language which filmmakers are learning and which audiences need to learn too.

3D can be used, for example, to make a scene appear more threatening or it can mimic a character's feeling of intimidation. It can introduce a disconcerting quality to a scene or perhaps induce a feeling of well-being—of being embraced by the scene. This is partially done on a subconscious level, you don't want the audience to necessarily notice the convergence, you just want them to be feeling it.

The skill of working in 3D lies in working out not only the effect of a single shot on an audience but considering the impact of shots either side of that shot and over the course of the picture.

It is important, for example, that a room looks the same size on the single as on the reverse, and on the wides as it does on the close-ups. At the same time though, it may be that the protagonist's house feels large and spacious at the start of the film when it is comfortable, safe, and his whole world, and then feels small and claustrophobic later on after travelling to far-off lands, at which point he is reflecting on how it pales by comparison to the palaces he has visited.

Equally, if there is a scene when the director wants more impact, then reducing the strength of the 3D leading up to that point will increase the impact after it, and if done correctly, through linking stereography, design, direction, and lighting, the more relaxed 3D prior to that point won't feel any less complete.

Working in stereo is about manipulating its feel over the length of the production in order to assist in the telling of a story, and ensure that the audience seeing the film in 3D will have a 'better' experience than if they had seen the film in 2D."

Basic Jargon

The stereoscopic medium is moving from a challenge focused around aligning dual cameras into one based on artistic choices. Already terms like "convergence," "interocular," and "screen plane" are forming part of the burgeoning new visual grammar, which might soon become as natural to filmmaking vocabulary as "close-up" or "racking focus."

While the industry continues to build 3D expertise, some technical jargon is unavoidable. Perhaps the most fundamental idea to grasp is that to match human stereo vision, two cameras need placing with their optical centers roughly 2.5 inches apart—the same interocular as human eyes.

Fig. 1.5 Does 3D have the power to connect to audiences in a way 2D cannot?

PINA, Azusa Seyama and Fabian Prioville © NEUE ROAD MOVIES, photograph by Donata Wenders.

"Much like the way that color and contrast in a film image is exaggerated to enhance the theatrical experience, the interocular distance, or more correctly, interaxial separation, is often increased to exaggerate the stereo effect, and add impact to the viewed image," explains digital film consultant Steve Shaw. "The problem though, is that it is not that simple in practice, as the impact of the stereoscopic image can be affected by more than the simple quantity of the stereo effect."

Since the main conceptual difference between 2D and 3D involves the addition of depth or space this requires some essential new terminology. For example, whereas in 2D filmmakers work only in terms of width and height, otherwise known as the x- and y-axis, working in 3D means they can also work with depth—or along the z-axis, which is also known as "z" space. Good composition and blocking of talent, props, or sets within "z" space is crucial to making the most of 3D.

The amount of 3D that emerges out-of-screen is known as "negative parallax"; the amount of 3D on-screen as "zero parallax" or the point at which the images converge; and the amount of 3D that appears into-the-screen is termed "positive parallax." Many filmmakers work with a depth budget, which is described as a percentage of parallax between near and far objects, behind or in front of the screen, and keeps the 3D within parameters that make for comfortable viewing.

According to stereographer Alain Derobe (*PINA*), "Audiences always want to be as close as possible to the action, but as soon as something comes out of the screen, to invade the auditorium, spectators withdraw in their seats, and they all become conscious that they're just 'watchers,' and realize that the element invading their space is nothing but a picture."

A new stereo language could get incredibly technical, wrapped up in calculus for measuring interaxial distances against focal length, determining the precise matching of lenses as they rotate and move through a zoom, or analyzing disparity values for every pixel.

However, many of the filmmakers we feature freely admit that they prefer to use more descriptive terms. Instead, to convey the effect that they want to achieve with 3D they use more descriptive terms such as "dial up" (or "dial down") the stereo, "punchy" (or "shallow"), "volume," "natural depth," "immersive," and "roundness," or simply "give me more (or less)" 3D.

A depth script, for example, is analogous to a musical score [see Fig 1.6]. It outlines the amount of 3D (the depth budget) at particular points in a script to underscore mood and emotion and to help tell the story. Broadly speaking, once you understand the emotion you want to achieve from the shot, you can think about how to use 3D to evoke it.

"Filmmakers are adopting a new language to describe how they want the 3D to work for a particular scene. But it is not an exact science and there is no creative industry bible you can refer to," says Jamie Beard, who worked with Steven Spielberg on *The Adventures of Tintin*. "Consequently, descriptions can be a little broad, often using a very emotional type of language, but nonetheless one that is understood in context.

"After all, people's interpretation of conventional film grammar can vary," he adds. "A two-shot for one person might mean framing from the hips, to another it can mean framing from the feet. In the context of the scene it is understood.

"So when talking about convergence on *Tintin* everyone understood what is meant by 'throw it back' or 'pull it closer' or when asking for the stereo to be 'more punchy,' or simply 'more stereo.' It doesn't need to get much more technical than that."

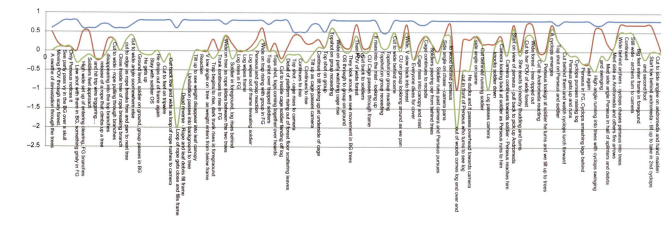

Fig. 1.6 An example of a depth script. The blue line represents the maximum positive disparity in the shot, the green line is the maximum negative, Image courtesy Chris Parks.

Vince Pace, Director of Photography and Co-Chairman, Cameron | Pace Group

Courtesy CAMERON | PACE Group.

"I've seen 3D go through different variations from being a gimmick that was extracted as a visual effect at certain points in a show to a more mature appreciation of what can be done when 3D is not treated as an add-on but embedded within a production.

3D should be viewed as a contribution to the artistic process in the same way that the presentation of lighting contributes to the overall vision. Jim Cameron, for example, spent as much time guiding animators frame by frame on lighting a scene in *Avatar* as he did on the 3D part.

A well-lit dramatic scene can only be enhanced with 3D presentation and I've never seen something that works in 2D, whether a battle scene or an intimate moment, that cannot be transferred equally into 3D.

However I don't want to make it sound as if everything is normal. The good directors and cinematographers understand the power that 3D brings to the table. The trick though is not to get overwhelmed by it. Don't make it the only trick a project has. Embed 3D in the creative process."

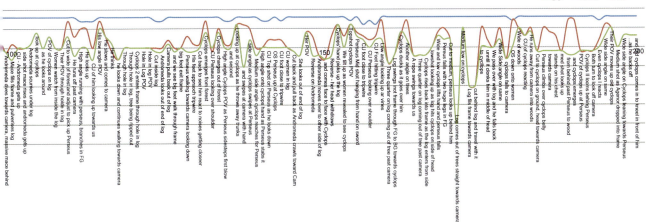

and the red line is the disparity of the main focus of the shot. This depth script is of one scene—broken down shot by shot as per the storyboard.

Making *Hugo,* Scorsese says, "I didn't use any technical language but rather my own emotional and intellectual response to the image. If I wanted to [push the 3D] further I would communicate that, or if there was something troubling me, I'd hold back. I would demand more or less IO [interocular distance]—I learned that. For me it was a question of how much more we could chisel away at the sculpture."

Exploring New Possibilities

Stereo 3D harks back to theatrical designs, literally staging in space, using the screen as a stage. This is nowhere more apparent than in projects such as *Carmen 3D, U2 3D,* or *Cirque du Soleil Worlds Away*, which are essentially 3D recorded versions of staged events. While evoking the concept of the proscenium arch, in which most of the action is staged behind the front of the stage with the audience looking directly on, the filmmakers have also placed the stereo cameras among the performers to generate a more intense and unique experience.

Not all theatrical events employ a proscenium arch. A circus, for example, is a natural theatre in the round. So too are many sports events. In Chapter 4 on live sports the team behind the production of the 2010 FIFA World Cup find themselves choosing camera angles completely at odds with the way football coverage is normally delivered. They are literally swapping sides, moving up and down in position to capture the best seat in the house. Does this present another avenue for exploration?

"In 2D you can't continually move up and down the stadia or swap sides or effectively change the viewer's seat in the stadium because in 2D there is no spatial awareness to guide the viewer," says Peter Angell, the creative director of FIFA's broadcast producer HBS. "In 3D the viewer instantly knew where they were on the field from the cameras we selected. That changed our perception of how different an experience 3D could be to 2D."

Fig. 1.7 The 2010 FIFA World Cup Final was captured live in 3D, the culmination of a groundbreaking 25-match outside broadcast.

Reproduced courtesy of HBS Group of Companies.

In *Avatar* a creative choice was made to create a window to another world by staging the majority of the action behind the screen plane. In the Parisian fantasy of *Hugo,* Martin Scorsese played with depth cues, pushing them to limits at times. Baz Lurhmann says he has staged *The Great Gatsby* using a similarly wide stereo range because he felt it suited his interpretation of the material.

By playing with the position of objects and characters either into or out of the screen filmmakers can begin to free themselves from the physical dimensions of the screen itself. What this means is that the "window" framed by the edge of the TV set or cinema screen can be dissolved from view and in effect becomes fluid or dynamic. Frames within frames can be explored.

The concept is incredibly powerful and has implications for how filmmakers might stage a scene in front and also behind the conventional screen plane. The traditional boundaries between audience and character can be removed with psychological impacts on the audience's perception of that character or narrative moment that have barely been explored.

The conventional wisdom is that stereo 3D should be cut more slowly than 2D since the 3D frame contains more visual information that our brain needs more time to resolve. Yet as numerous examples from *U2 3D* to *The Adventures of Tintin* show, there is no reason why fast cutting and camera movement or frequently changing camera angles can't work in 3D provided the shift in convergence is handled sensitively.

In *Avatar* the fast-paced action sequences tend to be choreographed using camera movement within the scene rather than multiple edits. "Your eye does need time to adjust to what it is looking at in the shot and follow the action," cautions Letteri. "In the real world, your eye can adjust instantly, but as filmmakers you have to make sure that you are giving the audience enough time to react."

American Cinema Editors (A.C.E) describes the editors' decision-making process as involving skills including storytelling, performance and shot selection, structure, rhythm, pace, length, taste, and talent.

Stephen Rivkin, A.C.E, who was nominated for an Academy Award for *Avatar* (alongside fellow editing nominees John Refoua, A.C.E, and James Cameron, A.C.E) found that "there were times, particularly in action scenes, where we realized that there might be too much visual information for the audience to take in while viewing any given shot. That led us to decide not to cut quite as fast. Rapid cuts in 3D don't work as effectively as shots which are allowed to run a little bit longer than you might normally."

Should the script demand it, a slower-paced approach might task the viewer to "edit" the scene by letting their eyes roam more carefully over the picture and within a scene rather than having a director focus attention on specific details by having multiple angles cut together through editing.

"You have to find a happy medium in films that play in 2D and 3D," Rivkin continues. "You don't want to slow something down so it is not as interesting in 2D, but you also

Fig. 1.8 Wenders: "I wouldn't even have started the film if it hadn't been for the arrival of 3D. We worked with prototype equipment on a prototype kind of a film."

PINA, Ditta Miranda Jasjfi in *Vollmond* © NEUE ROAD MOVIES, photograph by Donata Wenders.

want to be able to allow the 3D viewer to experience an action scene without being jerked around.

"Jim [Cameron] has this philosophy, which I completely agree with, that 3D should be an element of the story. It shouldn't be the star. 3D should be used to help create an immersive experience for the viewer without it being a gimmick or a distraction."

Eric Brevig, Director, *Journey to the Center of the Earth, William Tell: 3D*

Courtesy Eric Brevig.

"Audiences are beginning to realize when they see a film that is not necessarily crafted in 3D by design or that the director just didn't have the appetite or interest in using the stereo set of tools. They realize it is not the same as one in which the filmmaker made creative use of these tools.

At one extreme you can throw everything at the lens, at the other you can have a film that is nominally stereo but which barely leaves the screen plane. Both are valid and are a subjective choice based on the tone of the film. With a comedy you can get away with far more than with a drama which will only distract from the narrative.

As a director I will look for sets or camera angles in which there are many layers of depth to be able to show off the parallax between near and far but that's not to say I wouldn't do that in a 2D film either. I maintain that the best camera position for 2D is also the best in 3D but shooting in 3D you are also aware that your audience will have another layer, sometimes a subliminal layer, which adds to their involvement in the story.

This is because with 3D you have so much more visual information to help the audience feel involved in the scene. The filmmaker can conjure up an emotional connection to characters and story because the perception of depth triggers more of the neurons in the brain with which we experience real life.

My sense is that when watching stereo we are circumventing a lot of our defenses which we are used to using when seeing life reflected back to us on a 2D screen. If filmmaking is about suspending an audience's disbelief in a story then stereo helps us to achieve that. It can help us draw an audience into the story."

Beyond a Gimmick

"3D's image of being a gimmick gets harder and harder to defeat the longer there is no proof that it is capable of other things than just being a fairground attraction," says Wenders.

It is still early days of course, but filmmakers pushing at the technical limits of the medium are doing so with little to guide them. There is strong evidence to suggest that feature film grew as an art form by learning from other existing art forms—lighting from stills photography or perspective from centuries of painting. But as stereographer Simon Sieverts has noted, when it comes to 3D there is no context, no background to draw on except, perhaps, theater.

3D has yet to find its *Battleship Potemkin, Vertigo,* or *The Godfather,* all classic examples of drama, the one genre that is only just beginning to be exploited in the work of Ang Lee, Luhrmann, and Scorsese.

"Everybody thinks they know what 3D is for—for big action movies and science fiction worlds. But if you are already spending $200m on a movie to make it visually great the addition of 3D will improve it only slightly. If you spend only a few million on a production but you have a great script and great actors then the amount that 3D can improve your sense of being physically present and involved in that drama is huge. That is the piece that people are missing."

Those are the words of filmmaker Academy Award winner James Cameron, who has employed cutting-edge technology on stories that emphasize the perils of developing cutting-edge technology (*Terminator, Aliens, Titanic, Avatar*) [1]. He recognizes the creative impact that stereo can have on smaller-scale filmed stories.

"It's very frustrating that not enough filmmakers seem to view 3D creatively," says Scorsese. "Part of it is that mainstream cinema is an industrial system which makes 3D films for certain audiences. But I am 69 and I am unlikely to see a 3D film aimed at children—but I might go and see a 3D drama or a thriller."

Meanwhile, the filmmakers' toolset is evolving. Already the industry is moving toward filming and projection at higher frame rates and at higher resolutions with cameras capable of recording 8K, or four times the resolution of 35mm film.

Perhaps in the future technology will have advanced to the degree that it may be possible to capture (process, transmit, or project) images from multiple views, rather than the dual-eye view of stereo 3D. Perhaps technology will evolve to permit the capture of volumetric space using data from combinations of on-set cameras, or lenses comprised of multiple pixels (plenoptic), or infrared depth-sensing devices.

Research and development is continuing into all of these areas and when these technologies become practical perhaps filmmaking, or its successor, will have evolved to encompass the art of shaping light into new forms.

As Rob Legato, Oscar winning visual effects supervisor for *Titanic* and *Hugo* remarks, "Stereo 3D is the closest we will get to sculpture in cinema until it becomes holographic."

3D will remain a novelty while films and TV channels are sold on the hook of 3D alone. It will remain a novelty while audiences are fresh to its look and feel. One of the lessons that producers of 3D soccer broadcasts have found is that they must take the audience with them on the 3D journey. The TV narrative of a live soccer match is so engrained in the consciousness of fans that producers believe they risk alienating their core audience if a switch to a 3D mode of storytelling—different sets of angles, slower pans, and less frequent cuts—happens overnight.

Fig. 1.9 *Coraline* director Henry Selick: "We figured, let's ignore most of the rules and figure out what works for this film and how far we can push it."

"3D is a learned behavior," argues Hays. "If you were able to present any recent TV drama or feature film to an audience from the 1920s they may not be able to process everything that is going on from lip sync to camera angle because the grammar of 2D audio-visual storytelling has evolved so much. In the same way, the new grammar for stereopsis will take time to evolve in order to take the audience along with it."

At its best, stereo 3D can help create an immersive experience that enhances an audience's appreciation and understanding of mood and emotion or help convey a connection with an actor's performance, a landscape, or a narrative. It can inspire filmmakers to create stories that could not have been told in the same way before.

When pictures became talkies, when black and white became color, when widescreen formats were used in the cinema, and when high definition was introduced to TV transmissions, product was marketed on the back of each development. And each has become mainstream, fading into the background. Many believe this will happen to 3D too. By that point 3D will not be the reason to create, visit, or tune into a show but just part of what it means to enjoy being told a story.

"The artistic tradition goes as far back as storytellers performing around fires and inside caves," says Scorsese. "Storytelling, dance, sculpture and cinema are ways of reflecting an experience of life. 3D cinema is an extension of that because stereo vision is a natural part of the way we perceive the world.

"3D is an element to be used like sound and color but when new things are introduced there is always a resistance to change," he argues. "We are headed toward a day when 3D will be accepted as matter of fact just as color design, sound or the absence of sound is, but it will take dialogue between filmmakers to push and change the perception of 3D and to give it a new language while the technology will inevitably find a way to become less expensive. At a certain point 3D will be as inexpensive to use as color or the digital intermediate process and when it finds that level it will become normal."

3D as a Creative Force for Storytelling

Jim Chabin, President, The International 3D Society

"It's clear from any reading of the history of cinema that when technology is used to tell a story in a different way and consumers find that storytelling more compelling then the technology takes off.

When the industry went from talkies into sound, audiences were thrilled to hear actors speak. When we transitioned to color what caught fire was that film, and later TV fans, loved the opportunity to see their favorite actors or locations in color.

It is equally clear that with every breakthrough there has also been a baseline of resistance pushing back against it, simply because it is new and not well understood. We believe that visionary filmmakers must maintain focus and courage because such resistance can't be allowed to thwart the potential of a technology that enables a richer and more compelling motion picture art form.

3D has been around since the 1830s but it is only with the advent of digital technology that it can be used to help drive the story just as much and color, light, or motion.

The use of increasingly powerful computer chips throughout production is driving the ability to create with depth in a far more powerful and precise way than could ever have been accomplished during the last 150 years.

3D can now be used to explain or explore and thrill the viewer in ways that filmmakers have barely begun to touch on. We have the ability to create an environment where the viewer is taken into the story not just watching it.

To encourage the growth of 3D as a filmmaking craft there is a need for a handbook that focuses on the creative not just the technical, and for a glossary of terms that can help creative and technical filmmakers worldwide communicate so that everyone understands and feels more involved in the potential of stereoscopic motion pictures.

Many of our visionaries say they won't rest until they can see and hear Frank Sinatra in virtual reality in their living room. For now we have stereo digital 3D, a first step toward an emergent new art form.

The filmmaking community has learned to create stories by writing and reading scripts and storylines to determine camera angles and then scoring it with music, color, light, and dialog to create the most powerful and exciting piece of artwork we can.

Now we have the miraculous ability to give that material depth and a powerful realism because we can see figures in their full relief. Just as we score for every other filmmaking element we will compose in 3D to help us tell a story. It is a powerful new dimension of content creation and one of the most powerful developments in motion pictures since the beginning of film itself."

REFERENCE

[1] James Cameron in interview with Giardina and Pennington for the IBC Daily Executive magazine, p50, September 2011.

2

TOWARD EMOTIONAL DEPTH

IMAX had maintained 3D in its theaters since the mid-1980s but with a few exceptions, including nonfiction feature *Wings of Courage* (1995) and 2004's animated *The Polar Express*, the format was generally reserved for documentaries.

The current surge in mainstream 3D filmmaking began with the development of digital cinema projection systems, which could display a more precise 3D image than had previously been possible. The first studio to take advantage of this was Walt Disney Pictures, which opened the CG animated film *Chicken Little* in 2005 in 2D and on 84 freshly-minted digital 3D projection screens.

A limited number of 3D movies followed. This included Disney's stop-motion classic *Tim Burton's The Nightmare Before Christmas* (1993), which was converted to 3D and debuted in the format in 2006, as well as its animated *Meet the Robinsons* 3D release in 2007. In the same year, Robert Zemeckis' performance capture–based *Beowulf* for Paramount/Warner Bros. became the first Hollywood feature to open simultaneously in digital 3D and IMAX 3D.

In 2007 DreamWorks Animation CEO Jeffrey Katzenberg sent a strong message by announcing that, starting with 2009's *Monsters vs. Aliens*, all future DWA movies would be made in 3D. Soon, Disney announced that all its computer animated films, including those from Pixar Animation Studios, which it had acquired in 2006, would be made in 3D.

"When the audience experiences 3D and sees how exceptional it is—and the filmmakers understand how much greater an experience they can offer their audience—I think 2D films are going to be a thing of the past," Katzenberg asserted in a live 3D telecast to the 2008 International Broadcasting Convention in Amsterdam from the DreamWorks Animation campus in Southern California.

Interest in making 3D movies continued to build. Some live action movies produced in the format also arrived in digital 3D theaters, such as *Hannah Montana & Miley Cyrus: Best of Both Worlds Concert*, *Journey to the Center of the Earth*, and *U2 3D* (all in 2008). But at this early stage, it was largely CG animated films that were driving the digital 3D renaissance.

"It is not the animation specifically that lends itself to 3D but the way we create the shots," explains Phil McNally, stereoscopic supervisor at DreamWorks Animation. "In live action you have to get most of the settings correct in one take. It is 'live' after all. In our 'not live' world of CG we can go back and reshoot the performance over and over until we have a perfectly refined result. We are also free to move the CG cameras much closer to our 'actors' than would be acceptable or practical in live action. This allows us the use of wider lenses that can create better looking 3D."

Some of the filmmakers behind these early digital 3D films—already conscious that the potential of the format was something far greater than a limited gimmick—strived to use depth to support the emotional curve of the story.

"I think there is still a lot of territory to explore in 3D," says *Coraline* director Henry Selick. "3D doesn't have to be a gimmick, it can be something that can enhance the audiences' appreciation and understanding and emotional investment in the story. ... There has got to be a reason [for 3D] in the story, in the art direction and, emotionally."

"It is still so early in the process that I think if we get filmmakers who care about using this technology to really tell their story in a better way, people will connect with it," says Travis Knight, CEO of LAIKA, the animation studio behind *Coraline*.

"You can tell a story in a completely new way, and it is really exciting," Knight says. "You only come across these sorts of innovations once in a generation. I hope that filmmakers do not waste this opportunity and really use this medium and these tools to their fullest effect."

While the full promise of 3D has yet to be realized, creative exploration is well underway and lessons are being learned. For instance, Buzz Hays learned from his work as senior 3D visual effects producer on *Beowulf* and other 3D projects that more camera motion and less cutting can be more conducive to the storytelling than traditional coverage.

Fig. 2.1 Henry Selick (left) and Travis Knight.

"The effect of cutting in 3D, rather than letting scenes flow and having the action played out in front of the camera can sometimes be jarring to the viewer," suggests Hays. "This may have to do with our basic human instinct of regarding new surroundings (or in this case, new angles) cautiously, as we tend to want to reacclimate to the situation when presented with a new perspective. Cutting in 3D using 2D cinematic grammar can cause a tiny disconnect from the story as the viewer adjusts to the new perspective.

"It's not that you can't cut quickly in 3D but that you don't need to cut as much," Hays stresses. "You tend to want to regard the surroundings a little, to absorb that extra information. In real life we instinctively regard the closest objects to us first before examining the rest of our environment, so directors can use stereo 3D as a more natural way of discovering a scene.

He continues: "We are in effect editing the 3D scene with our own eyes since we are able to better understand the components of a scene in relation to one another because we are given greater depth awareness."

The Polar Express underscored this message. "It wasn't originally conceived as a 3D movie," says Rob Engle, who worked on the IMAX 3D version of the film. "But one of the interesting things about the way Bob [director Robert Zemeckis] works is that he tends not to cut as often as most filmmakers."

Engle relates that on The Polar Express—which follows the journey of a boy to the North Pole—the average shot lasted 7-8 seconds, "almost twice that of [many other] filmmakers.

"The reason that is important in 3D is that long cuts give the audience time to connect with what they are looking at before you put something else in front of them. In our normal lives, there is no such thing as a cut. … We are used to it as a cinematic convention, but in 3D, it can be very disconcerting. Because Bob likes these longer cuts, it gave audiences more time to get into the shot and look around."

Engle suggests that ultimately The Polar Express in 3D connected with audiences because it gave the viewer a "sense of being there—being in the train car with the boy, of seeing Santa Claus close up. The atmosphere, particularly the falling snow, gives you a sense of space."

McNally suggests that there is a time to add 3D and a time to dial it back, but that this is still largely misunderstood. "There is a misconception: people think 3D is going to gravitate toward action sequences that will be cool in 3D; it is not true," he says. "It can be, but typically the way we are making action sequences are still heavily based on 2D action sequences—we are using fast cuts, shaky camera, longer lenses—which all work against stereo space.

"In the quietest moments, you get to just look at the character, that is the power of the 3D," McNally adds. "One of the strongest shots that you can make in 3D is engaging in the eyes of the character that you have just spent however many minutes of the movie telling us who they are and what is happening to them."

CORALINE

Although the short In Tune With Tomorrow, directed by John Norling and first presented by Chrysler at the 1939 New York World's Fair, broke ground as one of the early examples of 3D stop motion, the first stop-motion animated feature to be conceived and lensed with the format in mind was Coraline. Released by Focus Features in 2009, the movie combined classic stop motion with an inventive use of stereoscopic 3D and went on to receive honors including Academy Award and BAFTA Award nominations.

Fig. 2.2 Coraline's real world is greyer, but she discovers a magic passageway to an alternate world.

© 2009 LAIKA, Inc. All Rights Reserved.

Based on the book of the same name by Neil Gaiman, the dark fantasy was told by director Henry Selick, who also wrote and co-produced with animation studio LAIKA, following two years of preproduction. The production itself involved the creation of more than 130 sets that were housed on the stages at LAIKA, and hundreds of puppets. For the central character alone, 28 different puppets were created.

Selick says he started to think about making *Coraline* in 3D as far back as 2004, before the first digital 3D system had ever been installed in a cinema for paying customers, after being intrigued by the work of his friend Lenny Lipton on development of what became the RealD 3D digital projection system.

Anxious to learn more, Selick invited Lipton to LAIKA to give a series of seminars about the format, which helped convince Selick that 3D was the right approach for *Coraline.*

Photography took 18 months and involved the use of a single-camera rig that would shift left and right, in order to photograph each frame twice—one for the left eye and one for the right eye.

Director of photography Pete Kosachik, ASC, says he initially assumed that they would set the interocular to the distance between the puppets' eyes, roughly ¾ inch. "It turned out even that was too much," he relates. "We were right down there in very small IO. I'm hearing this from the live action guys as well. They don't use a full human IO distance when they are shooting; they use a smaller one."

Alternate Worlds

Coraline tells the story of an 11-year-old girl who feels incredibly isolated when she and her parents move from Michigan to Oregon. But then she discovers a magic passageway in the house that leads to an alternate, more-inviting version of her life—a magical, colorful home complete with an "Other" Mother and Father. This seemingly wonderful world soon takes a sinister turn when the Other Mother reveals that she does not intend to let Coraline return to her real family.

This central plot point required the lead character to move between the two worlds that were effectively identical houses: her real world, which she finds restrictive; and an alternate world, which is very appealing at the start and then turns dangerous.

Fig. 2.3 Selick: "The aim [with 3D] was to immerse the audience in the story, rather than being something their attention is called to."

The filmmakers used *The Wizard of Oz* as an inspiration, and in particular the use made of color in the 1939 classic to differentiate between Kansas and Oz. "They did that so beautifully using sepia black-and-white for Kansas and a beautiful, bright, saturated Technicolor the moment they land in Oz," says Travis Knight, *Coraline*'s lead animator. "We were trying to achieve the modern equivalent."

The director relates: "In *Coraline* we had a main character who is unhappy in her normal life and who discovers an alternate version of that life through a magic door. I felt that I could use depth creatively to help separate the two in the audience's mind, but to do so in a more nuanced way than *The Wizard of Oz* — just as cinematographers use different lenses to create different physiological reactions. I didn't want to make it quite as clear cut as 'everything here is in 2D and everything there is 3D.'

"The aim was to immerse the audience in the story, rather than being something their attention is called to," he explains. "In the real world sequences, Coraline feels claustrophobic, as if there wasn't enough air in the room. To accentuate that atmosphere we built sets with less depth to them so that the space is literally crushed. We kept the

Fig. 2.4 The sets were identical, but the alternate world was built with greater depth.

3D low-key and further sought to convey her emotional state by paring back the visual stimuli in these scenes to a greyer, muted palette."

By contrast when Coraline ventures into the Other world for the first time, "your retinas are burning with the color," exclaims Knight. "There are rich purples and reds, pinks and blues, and the sets and the stereography go way back into the screen. It's an exhilarating feeling of freedom and depth. You understand immediately why this world is so appealing to her."

The filmmakers also aimed to keep the stereography in tune with Coraline's emotional state as the story unfolds. When Coraline's world is caving in on her, the stereo depth is very shallow. When she feels more of a sense of liberation they exaggerated the amount of depth behind the screen plane.

"Generally speaking, to create a claustrophobic space, I would use a longer lens and compress everything," Kosachik says of the cinematography. "To give a sense of greater space, we use wide angle lenses. That is what you would use in 2D movies as well."

As to the art direction, Selick devised two different sets for each of the rooms, one for each of the story worlds. "The real world kitchen, for instance, might be only two feet deep, but in the Other world the kitchen was deep, deep," he says. "The rooms were identical, but the alternate world was built with greater depth."

A key 3D moment is the first introduction to the Other world, which begins when Coraline opens a secret door in her new home and discovers a portal. She crawls into what is effectively a long tunnel that extends far back behind the screen, without an end in sight. The edge of the portal—swirling with bright blues, pinks, and purples—is at the screen plane. When she arrives at the end of the portal, she finds herself back in an identical room in her house—but it has been given more depth than the room in her real world.

"At the portal the 3D is used to punch a hole in the screen and make it super, super deep," says Selick. "When Coraline arrives at the other end of the portal, she finds herself in what at first appears to be the same room that she had just left—only it feels different. By adding depth we were trying to create this feeling of relief, as if to say 'I can breathe, I feel better.'"

Adds Knight: "We decided to have the portal go deeper into the screen as if it were pulling the audience into this other world. The set pulls away from the audience, so they get this feeling of being on a precipice with everything dropping away to emphasize that she is going into this deeper world."

Fig. 2.5 Coraline discovers a secret door.

Fig. 2.6 A portal takes Coraline to an alternate version of her world.

Fig. 2.7 The father's study in the alternate world.

The Father's Study and the Theater Performance

As an example of how they marshalled art direction, cinematography, and stereography to help create these alternate rooms, Knight describes Coraline's father's study.

"In the real world, Coraline goes to visit her father in this ratty, ramshackle den that he is working in," Knight explains. "We used a lot of forced perspective by building the set very shallow. It is feels cramped, humdrum, and unengaging.

"When she goes into the Other world, we had the twin of that set built deeper and we shot with an exaggerated 3D. Her father's study now has a piano and at one moment a pair of hands come out of it to emphasize that this is a bizarre world where things can happen at any moment. It is a bit of a thrill, but also hints that there's something not quite right with this world. That even something fun and exciting can be menacing."

Another sequence in the Other world introduces a performance complete with a trapeze act that the alternate Mother has created to try to lure Coraline into a trap.

Fig. 2.8 When Coraline feels a sense of freedom the sets were shot with an exaggerated use of depth into the screen.

Relates Knight: "One of the things we learned early on in testing the 3D process is that you can push it too far. Like going to a sadistic optometrist, overindulgence and misapplication of the 3D effect can be unsettling, dizzying, even painful. We found this out through a number of mistakes. But we thought, what if we used this effect purposefully? What if we embraced the effect and the concomitant sensations and put it to use in service of story?

"The trapeze scene was a perfect place for it. As Coraline and the gymnasts variously soar above the theater we used a variety of techniques to emphasize the action. By overplaying the use of 3D depth in particular shots, breaking the rules of the interocular and alignment settings, and combining that with dramatic camera moves, we created a vertiginous sensation in the viewer, akin to looking over the edge of a high rise.

"The idea is to put the audience in the same emotional state as Coraline. It highlights the excitement and delight our heroine is experiencing, creating a vicarious rush, so when we pull the rug out from under her in the very next scene, both Coraline and the audience feel the loss."

"It was a good place to use 3D," Selick says. "When Coraline gets picked up and pulled through the air, it was great to travel with her in three-dimensional space. We built a huge theater [in which to shoot the scene]. We had a wonderful real space to move the camera around."

A Sinister Twist

"It was never about one scene doing all the work, it was about one scene in relation to the other," Selick says of the film's approach to 3D. "When Coraline starts to find out that the Other Mother isn't so wonderful—and that the miraculous other world that the Other Mother has created for her is a trap—there are a number of scenes where we intensify the stereography by starting to move the 3D forward across the screen plane and to poke out at the audience. This is meant to make the audience feel uncomfortable, that things are not right and unbalanced."

The Other Mother also goes through several transformations from friend and savior at the outset and into a creepy figure by the finale. "The first time we see the Other Mother transform, we performed a morphing scene where she goes from almost a carbon copy

Fig. 2.9 The theater performance.

of Coraline's mother, replete with button eyes, to something that is tall and freakish," Knight says. "When we see her transform, she grows toward the ceiling. We have the camera down low and use a morphing technique to grow the puppet and at the same time exaggerate the 3D [by bringing it in front of the screen plane]. You get the sense that this is a very intimidating presence that is towering over both Coraline and the audience. By using 3D in that moment, it goes to the emotional state of Coraline and the audience." This unique stop-motion animation morphing sequence runs for 130 frames, or nearly 6 seconds.

"If a character was supposed to have some sort of personal power, we would bring them out of the screen a little bit," Kosachik says of the team's approach in this, as well as similar story situations. "If they were intimidating someone, the person being intimidated would be pushed back behind the screen."

The Other world is a finite one. It has boundaries, in effect it is a gilded cage. When Coraline tries to escape she reaches the edge of the created world—offering another unsettling environment.

Fig. 2.10 The Other Mother goes through several transformations.

"We had realistic-looking trees that start to deteriorate and fall apart," says Knight. "They become geometric patterns which look like an abstract version of a tree, then simple shapes, then nothing." The result: Coraline appears on a white background. "When you lack certain visual cues, it is very difficult to have a sense of depth and dimension, and it is very disconcerting."

In the climactic confrontation as Coraline tries to reenter the portal and return to her real world, the Other Mother transforms into a large bug-like creature.

"She effectively rips the world apart and you see it collapse into what amounts to a spider's web," says Selick. "We used a considerable amount of 3D [to bring characters in front of the screen and give depth to the room] as the floor falls apart and the web pulls down and Coraline falls into this spiderweb."

Once that world is pulled away, the background returns for a brief point to that unsettling white background. "That is the scene where we went off the chart [with the 3D]," says Selick. "That is when we made the 3D the most intense, the most forced. We put in you the middle of the web with Coraline and the Other Mother.

Fig. 2.11 "We broke most of the rules," Selick says.

"By the end of the film, we restore a little more depth to the real world scenes to suggest that matters are back in balance. She has a life that she accepts, and she realizes that her parents do love her."

Breaking the Rules

Selick admits that in making *Coraline* they broke most of the cardinal rules about shooting in stereo. None were broken with the intent to cause eyestrain, it was instead about story.

"Most of the rules we broke were established back in the 1950s when the 3D systems were more limited, when breaking the rules had more serious implications for eyestrain," the director explains. "You really needed perfect screening conditions. The new 3D projection systems are more forgiving.

"What really matters is putting things together and seeing how they feel for yourself," he notes. "We figured, let's ignore most of the rules and figure out what works for this film and how far we can push it."

A "rule" that the filmmakers ignored was that everything needed to be in focus. "One of the tools we don't want to give up is controlling the focus behind and in front of the subject. We want to draw the eye to where we want it to go." Kosachik says.

"If things are going to be kept in the foreground out of focus, just keep them dark. This works if you don't force the audience to look through things that are out of focus (i.e., trees or bushes) to see what is behind it; push them off to the side instead. It has to do with composition as much as anything."

Kosachik also believes that every shot doesn't need to be in 3D, and that can help to enhance the depth when it is used. "If a big 3D moment was coming up, we would precede it with a few shots that were almost not 3D at all.

"Also there are a lot of things that can be made to look like they are 3D, but they are really flat," he adds, citing as an example a foggy scene outside Coraline's house in the real world. "Fog was shot in 2D and layered in 3D space where you would expect to see it. If you put enough flat images one in front of the next, it starts to look like 3D."

HOW TO TRAIN YOUR DRAGON

When the use of 3D is discussed in professional circles, you'd be hard pressed to find a filmmaker that doesn't agree that DreamWorks Animation's 2010 animated hit *How to Train Your Dragon* set an exceptionally high bar. Acclaim is given in particular for the way the story is told using 3D in harmony with elements from script to score to create a touching, humorous and entertaining ride.

How to Train Your Dragon opened March 26, 2010 and grossed $495 million worldwide at the box office. The feature earned two Academy Award nominations, including a nomination for directors Dean DeBlois and Chris Sanders for best animated feature and a nomination for composer John Powell for best score.

The film also earned a string of additional nominations and accolades. At the second annual International 3D Society Awards, this 3D community honored *How to Train Your Dragon* for best animated stereo feature and best stereography in an animated feature.

This was only the second stereoscopic 3D release from DWA, whose CEO Jeffrey Katzenberg threw down the gauntlet in 2007, declaring that all of the studio's animated movies would be made in stereo.

DWA enlisted directors DeBlois and Sanders—a pair best known at that time as co-writers and co-directors of Disney Feature Animation's *Lilo and Stitch*, which earned a 2002 Academy Award nomination for best animated feature.

Fig. 2.12 Hiccup doesn't share his father's enthusiasm for hunting dragons.

"How To Train Your Dragon" © 2010, Courtesy of DreamWorks Animation.

With *How to Train Your Dragon*, the duo found themselves in unfamiliar territory as this was not only their first stereoscopic movie, but also their first computer animated movie.

Still, the pair was not without a net. DWA has already invested in developing a 3D pipeline and its first stereo movie—*Monsters vs. Aliens* (2009)—was already in production when they came on board to write and direct *How to Train Your Dragon*. And, DreamWorks Animation had already brought in some experienced pros including McNally—a respected stereo supervisor who had already compiled a list of 3D credits including the first digital 3D theatrical release, Disney's *Chicken Little* (2005) and the 3D version of 1993 stop-motion feature *Tim Burton's The Nightmare Before Christmas* (2006).

How to Train Your Dragon producer Bonnie Arnold related that even with the DWA brain trust, the team was apprehensive, as they very quickly realized that the 3D approach for *Monsters vs. Aliens* would not be appropriate for *Dragon*.

Monsters vs. Aliens was conceived as a comedic spoof of monster movies from the '50s—an earlier golden age of 3D—and as such, lent itself to the use of in-your-face 3D. "That was the convention of the film," Arnold said. "If we used the same technique (on *Dragon*) it would have been odd."

This is because in contrast, *How to Train Your Dragon*—which was loosely based on the 2003 fantasy novel of the same name by Cressida Cowell—was a dramatic comedy set in a fictional Viking village that was much more emotional in tone and epic in scope.

Initially, the directors were concerned about Jeffrey Katzenberg's 3D mandate. Recalls DeBlois: "[We were advised] you can't have dark scenes because 3D doesn't work very well in low light; no rapid cutting because your eye needs time to adjust to the 3D in every shot; no shallow focus because 3D is all about the deep focus; and 3D seems to work best with wide angle lenses. For Chris and I, our favorite film language is soft focus, long lenses, low light, and exciting action scenes with rapid cutting. We thought immediately that this tool is tying our hands."

Arnold recalled that for inspiration, the core team began to go as a group to see 3D movies—some of the earliest digital 3D movies at that time. The eureka moment came when they saw *Coraline*, which opened in early 2009.

"*Coraline* seems to violate all the rules that we were told you cannot violate with 3D, and when they did, they either dialed back the 3D or found ways around it," DeBlois says, explaining that this lesson was an important turning point in their approach to the movie.

Fig. 2.13 Directors DeBlois and Sanders were initially skeptical of plans to make the film in 3D.

"How To Train Your Dragon" © 2010, Courtesy of DreamWorks Animation.

"The Movie That We Wanted to Make"

"We made a pact that we would make the movie that we wanted to make and find moments for 3D, but not let it be the cart that leads the horse," DeBlois explains. "We knew that we had the flying scenes. That was the 3D guarantee. We knew we could make those scenes full of depth and wild and roller-coaster-like. Then we started looking at the rest of the film, from an emotional standpoint, to see if we could make it more immersive. I was skeptical in the beginning. I could only see the disastrous effect of it—which would be to spoil a completely involving moment [with 3D] by turning it into a theme-park trick."

McNally related that as an early test, he and layout supervisor Gil Zimmerman put together a sequence that was very literal of what the directors asked of them. According to McNally, that mandate was: "We don't want anything to hurt. We don't want anything poking us in the eyes or gimmicky.

"Then we also put together a version that we thought used stereo emotionally to support the story," McNally adds, noting that after the directors viewed both versions, they agreed that they preferred the latter. "They got the emotional impact that a viewer gets without knowing what was actually happening technically."

Recalls Arnold: "They really did a lot of test shots, and Dean and Chris were slowly convinced by (seeing) what we could do to make the experience feel more immersive

Fig. 2.14 The stereo, used in this scene to emphasize the girl's precariously high position, is organic to the story.

"How To Train Your Dragon" © 2010, Courtesy of DreamWorks Animation.

and not disrupt the storytelling. … The new way of thinking was that 3D is another amazing tool to create stories."

Many of the creative decisions about the 3D were made when storyboarding was finished and the animated feature was moving into layout. Throughout the movie, the filmmakers allowed the stereo to come and go in an organic way that would support the story, coming together with additional elements including lighting, framing, and music.

For select sequences, the team employed what is referred to as a floating widow, dynamic stereo window, or edge masking. Explains McNally: "If you think of the frame created by the screen or the aperture of the projector, in 2D it is just a black frame that surrounds your picture and everything is composed within it. In stereo, that is talked about as the stereo window because it becomes like a hole that is cut into the wall where you look through it into the world, and on occasion somebody might walk up to that window and lean in and reach out through the window into your personal space.

"I think of the window as a division between 'personal' space and 'world' space," he says. "The stereo window will be there by default with the masking of the screen in a theater. But it doesn't have to be just that. You can also put masking into the image itself, which means that the frame can float off the surface of the scene or even be pushed behind the screen."

McNally elaborates: "The floating stereo window is a masking which is not tied to the screen depth. The frame itself becomes another depth component, which can be in front of the character or behind the character. It makes the screen position irrelevant if it is produced properly because compositionally what you are talking about is the character relative to the frame, not relative to the screen."

That effectively means that stereo could make a character who is in front of the screen appear to be beyond the stereo window. "Anything behind the stereo window feels like it is the world's space," he says. "If you want to feel like we are in a character's personal space, you want the character to be in front of the frame. The frame can be pushed back optically so that it is beyond the screen."

Hiccup Meets Toothless

The protagonist in *How To Train Your Dragon* is a teen named Hiccup. While he is the son of Viking leader Stoick the Vast, he doesn't share his father's enthusiasm for hunting dragons. Still, he tries to win his father's approval and aims to slay one of these creatures.

"Early in the film, Hiccup shoots down his first dragon in a night battle," DeBlois relates. "The following morning, he searches for and discovers the downed dragon, who is still alive but whose wings are tied. The youth is anxious to prove himself in his father's eyes.

Fig. 2.15 Hiccup discovers the downed dragon.

"How To Train Your Dragon" © 2010, Courtesy of DreamWorks Animation.

"As he approaches the dragon, the pair lock eyes in an intense sequence. The dragon is fearful, yet menacing. Hiccup is conflicted as he pulls out a knife—he doesn't want to slay the dragon though he desperately wants to earn his father's approval. In the end, he cuts the bonds and sets a surprised dragon free."

McNally explained that the 3D planning started with defining the emotional arc of the scene, meaning that Hiccup suddenly realizes that he is in danger when he finds the dragon, reaches his emotional peak as he tries to muster the courage to slay the dragon, then feels disappointment as he realizes that he can't complete the act.

"At the beginning the stereo should look normal," McNally explains. "Normal … is what you have established for the movie. In our case, normal means when you look at the characters, they look like they have a fully rounded appearance in a space that feels natural. As the anxiety in the story rises, we were literally taking shots from around 30% depth—if normal is 100%—and ramping it up to 150% depth. So we exaggerated the 3D within the shot itself and within multiple shots across an arc.

"The stereo would literally be growing as the music and tension were rising. Since the situation is stressful the stereo is transitioning from flatter to normal to stressful. At the point Hiccup realized he can't go through with it and everything kind of dropped emotionally, we played those shots at 30%. It is as if the color has drained out of the shot—but the depth has drained out of the shot. We are trying to do it in a way that is not obvious to the viewer. … We wanted it to still look within the realm of acceptable depth, but we are subconsciously changing how the shot feels without the audience noticing. What the audience is feeling is rising anxiety, then a release of tension.

"Stereo can do stress really well," he adds, advising, "You can make a lot more stress in 3D that you can in 2D, but part of our challenge is to avoid that when you don't want that."

DeBlois continues to explain this scene, noting that when Hiccup frees the dragon, its leaps, pinning the young Viking to a rock. "We dialed the depth to be more intense with each shot so by the time the dragon is full frame, his snout and teeth seem to extend a little bit into the audience. You can feel this dominant creature; you can also feel his breath on your face. With Hiccup we dialed up the depth so he feels quite vulnerable—here is his neck and his face, ready to be bitten off should the dragon choose to do so."

Forbidden Friendship

In a pivotal, emotional point in the film, Hiccup and the dragon, Toothless, begin to form a bond in a sequence dubbed "Forbidden Friendship." Here, trust is built between the unlikely friends through a series of subtle acts. DeBlois describes this section as the movie's "Black Stallion moment," recalling the scene from the 1979 film featuring the boy and horse on the beach.

"We knew this was going to be our scene," DeBlois observes. "Hiccup approaches this animal who is wounded and hungry and brings this offering of food. To his surprise, Toothless regurgitates a portion of that meal to feed Hiccup. It is a little bit of this communion that is happening, but only on Toothless' terms so the moment Hiccup tries to touch him, he flies off to the other side the cove. Hiccup—being the resilient character that he is—continues to approach the dragon and the dragon continues to makes it known that he doesn't want the contact and keeps pushing him away. Finally Hiccup—dejected—goes and sits on the other side of the cove, giving the dragon the space to come over and by virtue of his own curiosity observe what Hiccup is doing. The tables are turned. We also wanted to set up this idea that this dragon has a certain amount of intelligence. The dragon can mimic movement, but has an opinion. [Soon] Hiccup finds himself in close proximity but with his back turned to the dragon. Hiccup closes his eyes and offers himself up by extending his arm halfway. It is up to the dragon if he wants to complete the coming together, so he does, and that becomes the culmination of the scene."

"The last few shots were increased incrementally in depth so the touch was the emotional climax," McNally explains. "There is a certain amount of anxiety at the start. We go to normal stereo, as they become friends and build up to the contact point. It was very specifically shot with the reach out of the hand. The stereo window is out in front of the hand at the start dropping back to make it feel like the movement coming forwards is stronger.

"It is raising the intensity of what is there. If done incorrectly it can be fighting what the other components are trying to do," he adds. "If you have a very calm sequence but your stereo is set very aggressively, it is like having really loud music—it is almost undoing work you are trying to do with the other components."

Looking back, DeBlois admits: "What we didn't anticipate was that some of the more subtle moments—such as when Hiccup first makes contact with Toothless—would be an especially 3D moment. In fact, we feared the bad version of it, where he would reach out and the hand would come into the middle of the movie theater. We thought that would destroy it. We wanted the audience to be a part of the moment, and not be reminded that they were an audience sitting in a movie theater.

"It breaks forward just a little bit," DeBlois adds. "When Hiccup reaches out his hand, he is not reaching into the audience but he is extending it beyond the screen. We wanted the 3D to come and go and not announce its presence. They were able to take peak emotional moments like the one when Hiccup first touches Toothless and bleed it in naturally, so that it started more or less as a flat image and as the emotion intensifies—as he gets closer to touching Toothless—so does the amount of depth.

"So it is brought on very organically and has as the effect of pulling you into the moment and then releasing you gently as well so it doesn't feel abrupt. As such, it actually mimics the emotional flow of the scene and the steps that Hiccup as a character was going through to make it more visceral, even in its most subtle form."

In Flight

In another scene in the movie, Hiccup takes his love interest Astrid for a ride in the sky on Toothless—just after she makes the surprising discovery of the friendship. "That was all about poetry and beauty and seeing it from Astrid's point of view," says DeBlois, noting that the scene had two distinct parts. "The first part of Astrid's flight is the wild ride

Fig. 2.16 The floating stereo window was employed in flying sequences. The team knew they could make these scenes "full of depth"

"How To Train Your Dragon" © 2010, Courtesy of DreamWorks Animation.

because if you are in her point of view, this is terrifying. She hates these things, she has been conditioned to kill them on sight, and she finds herself crawling on the back of one. And this dragon doesn't like her. Only when she yields and gives up that aggressive vibe does Toothless decide to take them on a beautiful flight. There is depth; you are up in the clouds, but it is not as heavy-handed as the front end of it. Even in that scene, dialing it down to something that is beautiful and poetic, it really became romantic [complemented by John Powell's score]."

The floating stereo window was employed in flying sequences. "Where a character might start close, we'd push the window behind them and as they turned and swoop away, we would pull the window forward as the character is dropping back in space," McNally says. "If it looks like they moved 20 feet, a stereo window could exaggerate it, making it look like they moved twice as far—without increasing the amount of strain [on the viewer]."

In contrast, scenes that didn't seem to benefit from 3D were kept fairly flat. "We didn't try to shoehorn it into scenes that didn't require it or didn't benefit from it or would cause optical problems," DeBlois relates. "Anytime a tool seems to take over the creative process, then I'm not in favor of it. ... If 3D is going to hold its value out there, it's got to be something that is intuitive to the story."

As an example of when they didn't push the 3D, he cited a scene where Hiccup is in his workshop having an uncomfortable conversation with Stoick. "That is a pretty flat scene as compared with the rest of the film. Depth is not helping there; it is about an estranged relationship. It's not bringing characters together; there is no emotional pull. ... It helped to make the characters feel a little bit alienated from each other by keeping it flat. That lack of 3D in that moment was a storytelling tool."

Stoick's Desperate Search for Hiccup

At the film's climax, the Vikings go to confront the dragons at a giant nest—where they meet for the first time their true enemy, a giant dragon feared by all other such creatures. As the battle begins, Hiccup and Toothless take to the air to fight this common enemy. At this point, Stoick realizes that his understanding of dragons—and his son—was incorrect.

When Toothless' tail is clipped, he and Hiccup fall from the sky. McNally describes the storytelling from this point: "After the final battle we are presuming the worst has happened; it looks as if they have died. We played the stereo very flat and a distance behind the scene in a way that we hadn't at any other point in the movie to make it feel like something isn't the same as it was before. The stereo also made it feel more remote in my opinion."

Fig. 2.17 Stoick the Vast.

"How To Train Your Dragon" © 2010, Courtesy of DreamWorks Animation.

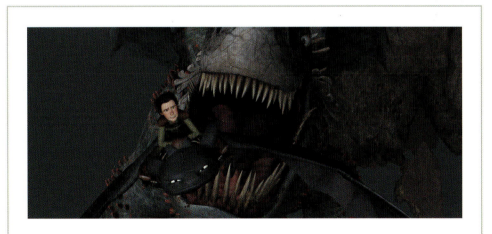

Fig. 2.18 Hiccup and Toothless in battle.

"How To Train Your Dragon" © 2010, Courtesy of DreamWorks Animation.

At this point Stoick's desperate search for his son ends when he finds a battered Toothless lying on the ground, and Stoick begins to grieve. But at that moment, Toothless slowly opens his wings, revealing that he had caught and protected Hiccup from the fall from the sky.

"During those waking up moments, the stereo starts to come back to life," McNally says. "Halfway through, the stereo returns to what we had established as normal. The lighting similarly reflects this arc.

"When you play it as a sequence you don't recognize that the beginning is flat or that it is deep at the end, but you feel that the story was sadder at the beginning and happier at the end. Everything works together—light, composition, animation, music—everything is in sync. The stereo is working in sync with the other components of storytelling."

Author's Note:

Following the film's success, DWA announced that it would make a trilogy based on How to Train Your Dragon. *DeBlois is writing and directing the second film, which was in production at the time of publication. Bonnie Arnold is returning as producer and Chris Sanders will also produce. A 2013 release is planned for the second film.*

3

PERFORMING ARTS: THE BEST SEAT IN THE HOUSE

A major part of the experience of watching a live performance at a concert, theater, or opera is about the tangible nature in which the performers can connect with an audience. Two-dimensional recordings of such shows have struggled to recreate that feeling but filmmakers have begun to show that by translating the space of the stage into a "virtual" space for a cinema or TV audience, something akin to being there can be achieved. The best attempts are far removed from any traditional idea of "filmed theatre."

Wim Wenders wrestled with the notion of translating the visceral body language of choreographer Pina Bausch's dance for decades before finding its expression in 3D. His acknowledged inspiration was the concert film *U2 3D*, which is still regarded as among the best examples of 3D live action of a staged event. As Steve Schklair, one of the film's producers, observes, a concert audience also wants to connect with their heroes on stage. The energy of a live show is derived from fans being within touching distance of their "gods" and even in vast stadia this relationship can become very intimate. The best 3D strives to achieve that electric feeling of proximity.

When Vince Pace and James Cameron were approached to help create a 3D film of circus artists Cirque du Soleil they realized they needed to revise the initial concept.

"The production team had a direction which was essentially to do a DVD in 3D and they were putting cameras where there would normally put 2D cameras and planning to cut it together as if for 2D," explains Pace. "If you are trying to recreate the physical experience of being there then you have to go about it a different way. In order to give viewers the opportunity of connecting with the artists you can't just shoot the performance from the back of the stalls. Here was a once in a lifetime opportunity to connect an audience to the incredibly visceral live entertainment experience of the Cirque du Soleil and simply presenting the performance for 2D cinema would not have the same power."

With James Cameron acting as lighting cameraman (and Executive Producer) on the project directed by Andrew Adamson, cameras were placed on the stage, among the performers themselves, and at times 90 feet above the floor.

Stereo 3D presents the opportunity of a "staged space" behind and in front of the motion picture screen. This is literally apparent in the filming of ballet, theater, or music and was at the forefront of director Julian Napier's mind when preparing a feature of the opera *Carmen* in 3D. He believes in the importance of staging objects and performers along the z-axis as a more powerful means of leading the eyes and directing the attention of the audience rather than through cutting or selective focus.

Aside from the obvious similarities between these projects as 3D films of staged pieces, there are perhaps less obvious parallels to draw. Napier makes considerable use of Steadicam on stage to bring the audience into the action, particularly at intimate moments. In the same way Wenders takes his camera on stage so that in a scene from the performance *Le Sacre du Printemps* the dancers interact with the lens as if the technology is a performer, not an interloper.

U2 3D is a darkly lit film in which the concert's stark lighting design was largely kept intact, a stylistic device that in stereo makes the foreground figures stand out sharply from the background. Although he films several pieces outside the theater, Wenders too favors this approach for the stage pieces giving *PINA* a modern, painterly look.

It is claimed that *U2 3D* pioneered the use of multiple layers in its construction while the editing uses cleverly composed dissolves to rapidly transition between shots. Napier may not have been influenced directly by this but he also uses transitions rather than cuts to build his story and keep the disparity on an even keel.

The projects featured here are driven by music with Napier and Catherine Owens, the director of *U2 3D*, conscious of constructing a narrative arc according to the drama of the arias or songs. Wenders too ensured that the music to Pina's dances was present at all times so that it contributed to the rhythm of each shot, especially for the outdoor sequences, which were all shot on Steadicam.

More than that though, Owens says she was acutely aware during *U2 3D* that the negative space between the audience and the on-screen (out of screen) band members was inhabited by audio.

Fig. 3.1 *PINA* was conceived by Wenders in 3D as the only cinematic means to understand Pina Bausch's way of looking at the world.

PINA, Rainer Behr © NEUE ROAD MOVIES, photograph by Donata Wenders.

"When you are crafting for depth space everything from the glasses of the person on the seat to the back of the frame comes into play," she says. "Filmmakers must try to understand how this whole new space impacts on the audience psychologically. Since 3D is an illusion and doesn't exist until our brains form it every bit of information you give it will help them form a certain impression of the scene in front of them.

"A crucial part of the strength of the 'illusion' is the audio as we also 'see' in our mind's eye through what we hear," she continues. "We spent as much time crafting this space as we did on the picture. While there was not a single overdub on the film, we deconstructed each song, focusing on the stems of each instrument and vocals in order to place them back into the correct 3D context for the visual image they were married to.

"For example on *Sunday Bloody Sunday* where Bono is singing to camera and you can also hear Edge singing off camera, as Edge is normally stage right of Bono we took that vocal and placed it only on the left side of the screen, so while you see Bono your mind can also 'see' where Edge is by the direction of the audio.

Fig. 3.2 Catherine Owens, director, *U2 3D*: "Filmmakers must try to understand how this whole new space impacts on the audience psychologically."

© U2 Limited.

"These actions while small in themselves add to the many nuanced layers and strong impressions you can create in 3D. The more you understand that space the more of your imagination you can bring to it."

Wenders realized that the soundtrack initially mixed for *PINA* simply didn't work when played back over the 3D visuals. "It had been conceived in 2D, and that was audible. We had to open up all the files again and restructure the audio space. The mix had to become more 'transparent.' Since 3D is guiding your eyes so much more than 2D, it became necessary to adjust the mix to what we actually saw, and what you therefore needed to hear better."

For Wenders, depth is a phenomenon that the present cinematic audio environment in cinemas cannot yet match, although moves to introduce 7.1 and beyond surround systems may provide an answer.

He went through considerable efforts to produce the best possible two-dimensional print so that *PINA* could also be shown in smaller cities without access to a 3D screen.

Wenders personally color-corrected the 2D print and saw it several times noting that the advantage of the 2D version was a higher overall sharpness and definition—resolution that, he says, inevitably gets lost in the 3D process.

"The disadvantage is that the 2D print was exactly what had kept me from doing this film for so long," he says. "Something essential was missing here, and each time I saw the mono print, I was reminded of it. The very element in which Pina had been working, the depth of her stage, wasn't there. The language of her art, defined and expressed by the bodies of her dancers, was indicated, but strangely pale. Seeing the mono print, I am each time reminded of the invisible wall that separates dance from the (conventional) screen.

"Pina's artistic invention 'Tanztheater' (dance theater) has an incredible freedom and lightness of being. On a two-dimensional screen it loses some of that. *PINA* was not only conceived with 3D in mind, it would never have been made any other way. It was started with the conviction that 3D was the ideal and only language for it."

U2 3D

In many ways a conventional concert film, *U2 3D* eschews B-roll backstage footage and interviews to concentrate on recreating the experience of watching the band's live perfor-mance during the Vertigo tour of 2004-06.

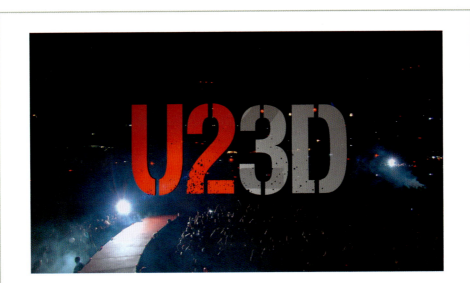

Fig. 3.3 Shot in 2006 and released in 2008, *U2 3D* is still regarded as one of the best examples of 3D live action. © U2 Limited.

The film began life as a creative experiment for U2 and by directors with no 3D experience.

Today, Sony screens songs from the movie as part of its training courses for stereographers and cinematographers at its 3D Technology Center in Culver City.

U2's art director Catherine Owens was instrumental in getting the project off the ground. She realized the potential of the new format after being shown test clips of NFL matches produced in 3D by equipment developers Cobalt Entertainment, founded by Steve Schklair.

"U2 are always keen to have a sophisticated conversation about their live shows and they were open to the idea that 3D was a natural extension of their live presentations to date and would be a perfect format to document the pure performance," explains Owens, a long-term collaborator with the group having art directed the band's ZooTV in 1992 and subsequent tours PopMart, Elevation, and Vertigo. "The aim of the film was to keep all the emotion of the performance intact, the relationship between the band on stage and the band's relationship with the audience and let that be the only concept."

After showing them a short 3D reel she made of the band at the beginning of the Vertigo tour, Owens convinced U2's members to agree to a feature length 3D concert film, which she would co-direct with Mark Pellington (an experienced feature film and music video director credited with work for INXS, Pearl Jam, and U2's *One* video). Owens had little directing experience but she could draw on her expertise in sculpture, video art, sound design, and photography.

"I worked with U2 on the video for *Original Of The Species* (2005), which married 16mm live action film with animation and motion capture, and was a precursor for what we did on *U2 3D*," she says. "A lot of my personal drive is to give technology emotion, so it's trying to crossover those two worlds. I'm well-versed in performance art and video so that was my inspiration."

In early 2004, preproduction for *U2 3D* was begun by 3ality Digital (now 3Ality Technica), a company formed from Cobalt Entertainment and partners including *U2 3D* producers Peter and Jon Shapiro. Nominally staged around one night in Buenos Aires, the film was shot at seven locations including Sao Paolo, Brazil and Santiago, Chile using up to nine pairs of cameras at any time over two years.

The Intimacy of Live Performance

"Because I had a long-term relationship with the creative direction of the live shows my approach to *U2 3D* was to treat it as a theatrical production where the band are

Fig. 3.4 The film's signature 3D moment in which Bono reaches out to the audience, presented in strong negative parallax, was captured on a test shoot prior to filming.

© U2 Limited.

the performers, the songs are the script, and everything on stage is part of the set," Owens explains. "My intuitive feeling for 3D was that it was a virtual reality where you can be immersed in a performance. I guess I took this idea literally since we referenced [Steven Spielberg's] *Minority Report* in our initial design, and specifically the sequences where Tom Cruise is interacting with a virtual computer screen. In that film you accept that what you are seeing as reality—and that is what I wanted our film to feel like. I wanted to include animated overlays but in such a way that the audience wouldn't notice, instead accepting that these VFX are part of the on-stage performance."

This most memorably manifests itself in a sequence during *Bullet the Blue Sky* where Bono bends down and mimes dialing a telephone. Later, in post-production, a telephone was animated to fit the sequence and then animated to transform into a newborn baby with the cord of the phone developing into an umbilical cord held in Bono's hand.

"The animation is also created as a reflection in Bono's glasses, which is almost subliminal in its appearance in the film, but crucial because I think it makes the virtual reality of that scene appear a natural part of the performance," explains Owens.

That moment was one of a handful where the band members appear self-consciously aware of the 3D cameras, according to Owens who had explicitly directed U2 to ignore the cameras and perform as normal except in instances where the muse took them.

"We saw a lot of IMAX science-based 3D films before embarking and were adamant that what we did not want were gimmicky in-your-face actions," she says. "You can get away with it once or twice if it appears natural but it just looks forced and incredibly tiresome otherwise.

"U2 have their own clear but minimalist language on stage and so the only direction was that they should be a little more conscious of their own language between the groups

Fig. 3.5 Multiple rigs were used including some from Pace (now CPG) and 3Ality, here shown fitted with Sony HDCF950 CineAlta digital cameras and Zeiss zooms.

© U2 Limited.

they form on stage. That worked well because I think it took everybody away from feeling like they had to perform, so in those one or two moments where the band break through, it's enough. I wanted to get those small personal relationships that they have and present it on an extra scale. Bono took this on board but I also said that if you find yourself in a moment and you feel you can give more, then feel free to do so."

The second moment, and what has become the signature clip from the film, was captured during a two-day practice run of a show filmed in Mexico City for the crew to learn the choreography of U2's performances. During *Sunday Bloody Sunday* Bono reaches toward the camera, his hand inches from the lens, which emerges from the screen at a fairly extreme 5%-6% angle of negative parallax. It is an intimate moment but like the rest of the footage wasn't rehearsed.

The shows were filmed without storyboards or shooting scripts to ensure footage of U2's performances was improvised. Rather than being directed, U2 performed each of

Fig. 3.6 Peter Anderson, one of the show's two cinematographers.

Image courtesy Steve Schklair.

their concerts as usual, with the crew capturing footage in real time for the full 2 ½-hour concerts.

Going against the grain of conventional promo and concert filming, Owens also opted to retain the show's generally dark but striking lighting design and used the arena's shadowy and dark areas to enhance the feeling of intimacy that the audience has with the band.

"Conventional lighting for concert films is often too bright and this means washed out performances and no atmosphere," she says. "So we lit the film using the show's own lighting scheme so that when audiences are sitting in a darkened cinema space the incredible atmosphere comes through.

"In the song *Miss Sarejevo* we used a distant shot of the audience in the dark but holding up lights from their cell phones to create this incredible wave of light. A 2D director would not have lingered for so long but it seemed perfect for the slow pace of that song."

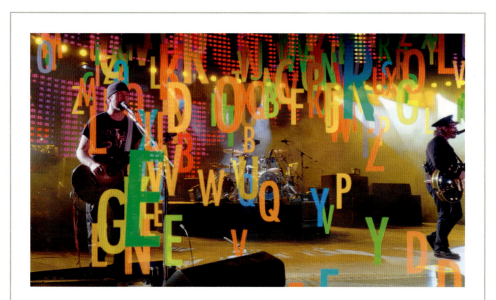

Fig. 3.7 The track *The Fly* was highlighted with animation, layered in 3D.

© U2 Limited.

Schklair says each concert was treated like a live outside broadcast. "Filming concerts are all about capturing performance and although we didn't know the exact details of what was going to happen we could prepare ourselves for the key moments of performance in each song," he says. "Part of the experience of being at a concert is the interaction the band's members get with the audience by moving about the stage. The best way to capture that movement is to use something that shows space, so that if a band member goes to the back of the stage we feel them walking away from us and if they move to the front we bring them to the front of the screen plane or sometimes in front of it.

"They should feel as close to a cinema or TV viewer as they did for an audience at the front row of the concert. You can't get that understanding of choreography in 2D because the band are always in the same place in space."

Fig. 3.8 The film was kept intentionally dark and lit largely using the live show's own lighting scheme to retain atmosphere.

© U2 Limited. Photograph by Taylor Crothers.

U2 harbored doubts that the slow pace of 3D would make their performance look cumbersome or uninteresting, especially when contrasted with their previous concert films and promos which typically involved fast cuts between shots.

"I instinctively felt that we should take a more collage like approach and use layers to dissolve between frames so that we transition quickly from the screen plane to behind the screen plane rather than use hard cuts," says Owens.

Many of the transitions were created by layering several frames of footage on top of one another into composite images. Each of the layered frames featured a different depth of field to enhance the 3D effects, and up to five images were layered together in a single shot. Several shows were edited together to create one performance; with Owens strict in ensuring that U2 wore the same clothes every night to maintain continuity.

"In one shot, we have Larry in the background and the Edge layered over Larry, and Adam's to the right and Bono's in front," says Owens. "Two of those layers came from a completely different image, and the image behind and in front stayed in the same space. If you want you could move the front image out and bring a new image in and keep the two images in the middle space exactly the same. That's made up from two or three different shows, just that one little moment."

Editing *U2 3D*

According to Schklair *U2 3D* also debunked the idea that 3D means you can't do rapid cutting. "At the time that was the accepted myth because it was felt fast edits would pull the audience's eyes in too many different directions too fast for them to adjust. Yet *U2 3D* was edited to incorporate dissolves of at least four frames between shots. The issue is not that you can't do fast cuts, the issue is that you can't jump depth quickly.

If the depth is level from shot to shot and the subject you are converging is at the same depth shot to shot [manipulated in post] then the audience is not being forced to adjust their eyes. Directors and editors need to be able to use fast paced sequences to tell the story and I think *U2 3D* showed them that it was possible in 3D."

With editor Oliver Wicki, Owens took more than 100 hours of footage and segmented off the "good" long, medium, and close-up shots to begin the process of collage. She also decided to choose 14 songs each around five minutes' duration and to give each an identity [one crowd based, another guitar based, one with the whole group, another just on Bono or on drummer Larry Mullen, and so on]. Each song was then identified as heavy, medium, or mellow in pace and character.

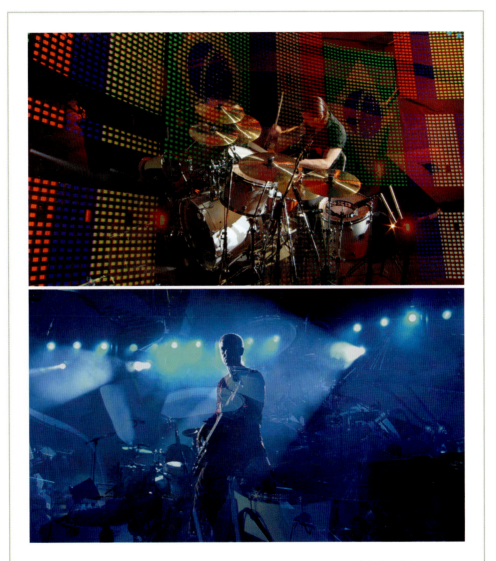

Figs. 3.9 and 3.10 *U2 3D* featured the use of multiple layers in its construction while the editing uses cleverly composed dissolves to rapidly transition between shots.

© U2 Limited.

"Once these identifiers were in place we built an arc from the beginning to end and within that we were able to give each song its own look for 3D, so I felt we were able to keep reintroducing 3D without using any particular gimmicky tricks but keeping the feeling natural to the song, the performance, and the whole narrative," she says.

"3D is like working with clay, since it has more dimension than a mere 2D surface, it is malleable, soft in ways and tricky to get the whole piece working continuously as one.... Like clay it is unforgiving and if you don't know how to work it, or you try to impose too much onto it, you will end up with a messy lump.

"From an artistic point of view you can use 3D to shape a concept on many levels at one time. It is not just about telling an audience something and hoping they will like what you are saying, its more about shaping a feeling so that when they leave they leave moved by the experience of having been drawn into performance."

PINA

Wenders planned to translate Bausch's art from stage to screen since first seeing her perform 20 years ago but always hesitated because he didn't know how it could be achieved.

"I realized my craft had its limits and that some of the glory of her dance theater would necessarily be lost in translation," he says. "I saw lots of other dance films, from the past, and they all confirmed my suspicion: there was a translation problem between dance and film, something like an invisible wall that separated the live experience from the screen. The tools of my craft somehow couldn't break that wall down, or transcend it."

The moment of epiphany came when watching the *U2 3D* premiere in Cannes in May 2007. "As soon as the film started I knew that was what I had been waiting for," Wenders recalls. "*PINA* became a 3D project immediately. I called Pina from inside the festival hall, as soon as the credits were over. I didn't have to explain much to her. 'I think I know how to do it now!'"

Wenders describes the experience of watching *U2 3D* as that of a huge door opening in the screen and it became obvious what had been missing: space, the element that dancers conquer with each gesture, each step.

"All of a sudden, space was available as a new film language," he remarks. "That was a huge realization. While I was watching *U2 3D* all I really thought of was the affinity that

Fig. 3.11 Wim Wenders and dancers of the Ensemble of *Le Sacre du Printemps* shooting *PINA*.

© NEUE ROAD MOVIES, photograph by Donata Wenders.

3D was going to have for dance, and vice versa. That seemed so obvious. The invisible wall could be cracked. I didn't know how exactly, I just had blind faith that this was the solution."

Wenders and Pina Bausch began planning a 3D film together. The broad concept was to stage and film four pieces (*Le Sacre du Printemps*, *Café Müller*, *Vollmond,* and *Kontakthof*) at the Wuppertal theater, and that was only possible if there were public performances. That pushed principal photography back to the fall of 2009 when, on June 30, 2009, Pina Bausch died suddenly of cancer.

"Her death was unimaginable, and it came totally unforeseen, to her family, her friends, her company," says Wenders, who cancelled the film despite having conducted a series of test shoots. "It seemed like there was nothing else to do. The concept I'd written was based on her presence in front of the camera, and on her being behind it with me. It was

Fig. 3.12 Wim Wenders: "All of a sudden space was available as a new film language."

PINA, Azusa Seyama, Andrey Berezin, and dancers of the Ensemble of *Le Sacre du Primtemps* © NEUE ROAD MOVIES, photograph by Donata Wenders.`

going to be a film about Pina's gaze. I wanted to explore how she looked at the world and what enabled her to decipher body language like nobody else before her."

The entire film was an effort to help people understand Pina's way of thinking and her way of looking at the world. "Pina was not a talkative person, she did not trust in language very much," says Wenders. "So we did not rely on words either, but tried to make a film that was based on visuals. 3D would allow us to understand the architecture of her choreography so much better than a flat recording."

When the dancers started to rehearse the four pieces that were going to be performed, as planned, in October and November 2009, it dawned on the director that canceling the film might have been the wrong decision. Pina would have wanted these pieces to be filmed, he thought, and her eyes were still on all of them.

"The film with Pina was no longer possible, but together with her dancers we could make a film for Pina. So we jump-started the project, on very short notice, just to record those four pieces in their entirety as a first step.

Fig. 3.13 Wenders believed 3D would allow audiences to understand the architecture of Pina's choreography far better than a flat recording.

PINA, Wim Wenders, Ruth Amarante, Andrey Berezin, and Jorge Puerta Armenta © NEUE ROAD MOVIES, photograph by Donata Wenders.

An Ominous Start

In preparation, Wenders saw as many 3D films as he could but found the experience unhelpful since most projects at that time were animated. *Avatar* was still a few months from release. He needed help and at first turned to his next door neighbor in Berlin, François Garnier, a French computer graphics tutor at Paris' Ecole Nationale Superieur des Arts Decoratifs. In turn, he introduced Wenders to Alain Derobe, a cinematographer turned stereographer and 3D rig designer with credits for stereo features *Safari3D* and *Camargue* under his belt [1].

"The first thing I told Alain: 'I don't want an effect-driven 3D. I want a very natural look for the film I have in mind. A sort of 3D that would make itself forgotten after a few moments. The attraction of our film has to be Pina Bausch's art, not the technology with which we are recording it.' Alain looked at me and waited for quite a while until he answered with a question: 'How long do we have until the film starts?' I only understood what he meant when we did our first tests."

The tests were a disaster. As much as Wenders felt 3D was able to open up space and introduce depth as a new cinematographic language, it had huge flaws in another area: they struggled with rendering fast movement.

"We needed depth, of course, and that had been the thrilling discovery with 3D. But movement was just as important for dance. If we couldn't represent movement elegantly, we wouldn't be able to proceed."

When *PINA*'s 3D producer Erwin Schmidt walked in front of the camera waving his arms, "on playback he looked like a multi-armed Indian Goddess... while the camera assistant running around in circles had many legs," he recalls.

"I couldn't possibly show this to Pina. They contradicted sharply to the glorious things I'd been telling her about 3D. The technology wasn't quite where I had imagined it to be. It had some clear drawbacks."

Nonetheless he proceeded to prepare for the film. Each of the four pieces was recorded over a week of four to five public performances each, with an additional couple of days where the production had the dancers and stage to themselves.

Since the public performances had to be shot without interruption the crew prepared for shooting takes up to an hour long. Garnier and Wenders learnt the pieces almost by heart, and devised an "itinerary" for camera position and movement.

"We needed to know at any given moment of each piece where exactly the ideal placement of our main 3D rig was," explains Wenders. "That main camera position was defined by the reach of a huge Technocrane, which could reach from about the center of the auditorium to the middle of the stage." (Actually, it was positioned left of center for two of the performances, and right of center for two. The Company could only sell tickets for half the auditorium, the other half was blocked by filming equipment.)

"I felt like I discovered each piece from scratch and started to understand their elaborate spatial structure so much better," he explains. "It was really like you could be at the ideal point of vision for each moment, which even beats the experience of a live performance where you are usually locked up in your seat."

A true-to-scale floor plan of the stage was drawn for each of the four sets, with a grid then laid over this map. With videos of each piece, mostly wide shots, Wenders and

Fig. 3.14 When filming started in the fall of 2009, the available 3D rigs were still quite large to get close to the dancers on stage. Consequently a Technocrane became the main tool.

PINA, dancers of the Ensemble of *Le Sacre du Printemps*. © NEUE ROAD MOVIES, photograph by Donata Wenders.

Garnier knew at any given moment where the dancers were on the stage. And with the help of an inclinometer (an instrument for measuring angles of slope) they could work out where the camera should be positioned for the best possible spatial impression.

"We knew when the crane had to withdraw (because it could never be in the way of the dancers) and when we could advance onto the stage," he explains. "We drew up an itinerary for each piece, consisting of hundreds of camera displacements. That was our storyboard, so to speak. When we shot, the two guys who operated the crane became our main collaborators. One was panning the arm, the other one was working the telescope extension, and they both had internalized our grid so much that they knew it by heart.

"[director of photography] Hélène Louvart was operating the remote head, I was talking to her and to our two crane operators like a madman, always trying to tell the three of them in advance where to move next, while François saw everything live on a 3D monitor and gave me feedback about the 3D aspects of the shoot."

This live shooting aspect, which Wenders says he has had no previous experience of, was he admits "really nerve-wracking" but because he and Garnier had internalized the pieces, "we were extremely well-prepared."

Fig. 3.15 Wenders collaborated on the stereo design with director of photography Hélène Louvrart, stereographer Alain Derobe, and stereo consultant François Garnier.

PINA, Hélène Louvrart and Wim Wenders with dancers of the Ensemble of *Le Sacre du Printemps*. © NEUE ROAD MOVIES, photograph by Donata Wenders.

On the days that the crew had the stage to themselves they worked differently. The crane was brought to the edge of the stage, to extend its reach into the stage, and Wenders concentrated on select moments he wanted to cover with close-ups that were not possible during the public performances.

"In both cases, the new thing for me was to consider the entire depth of each shot, each volume of space the cameras were capturing. The inclinometer was helpful with that. I began to form an impression about what was in the foreground and background of each setup. We used two different focal lengths in preparation, two different angles and therefore two inclinometers."

Fig. 3.16 During the shoot Garnier sat in front of a 3D viewing system consisting of two big LCD monitors, set up at an angle of 90 degrees, with a semitransparent mirror between the two allowing live 3D control.

PINA, François Garnier, Wim Wenders, and Robert Sturm © NEUE ROAD MOVIES, photograph by Donata Wenders.

Directing "Natural Depth"

Wenders states: "We basically shot the entire film on sets of Zeiss Digiprime lenses of 10mm and 14mm focal lengths (about 80% was shot on 10mm, about 20% on the 14mm) because we felt that they corresponded most to our human vision. In the edit it proved also more pleasant if you weren't changing your field of vision with each cut."

Wenders' 3D concept was to achieve a natural, pleasant feel that would as closely as possible represent a human point of view for each new camera position. This approach also synchronized with that of Alain Derobe, who had refined a 3D methodology he calls "Natural Depth".

"This method focuses on the space that the characters are supposed to occupy, in relation to the story," explains Derobe. "It never gives any unjustified stereoscopic advantage to a specific character, even if the most famous movie star is playing the part. We never converge to anybody in particular, but precisely to the place that gives the audience the most coherent sensation of depth, and in which they will easily find their way."

He adds: "Whenever 3D is of secondary nature, not essential for the storytelling, then it has to stay in a safe background or on the screen plane to give some rest to the audience's eyes. I always ask my crew not to do any stereoscopic calculations. Formulas, tables, software never consider the image composition, which for me is essential."

When it came to camera placement the team realized that lateral movement was fine, so long as it wasn't too abrupt. A slow lateral movement was found to increase the depth perception and Wenders used this technique in preference to static camera positions.

Fig 3.17 With DP Hélène Louvrart, Wenders ruled out anything longer than 20mm—and even that was used rarely.

PINA, Hélène Louvrart © NEUE ROAD MOVIES, photograph by Donata Wenders.

"Moving forward (or backwards) also worked really well for 3D," he explains. "And even fast lateral movement became acceptable, if you were able to attach the movement exactly to a movement of dancers. Fast lateral moves that were not following a movement on stage were disastrous. Our camera placement was largely dictated by the choice of the 10mm and 14mm lenses. This meant we also avoided the time-consuming lens changes that always meant that the rigs had to be completely recalibrated.

"Usually, one rig was equipped with one focal lens, the other rig with the other, and we shot with both rigs simultaneously. But apart from that I also felt that cuts worked better and that depth perception was more pleasant to the eyes if we more or less stuck to one focal length."

Much of *PINA* was shot in positive parallax—as if to extend the stage from the cinema audience into the screen and to maintain a naturalistic feel. There are occasional moments when objects are converged out of the screen in negative parallax.

The first instance is in the beginning when the dancers wander off into the back of the stage and they continue their dance behind a transparent curtain. The camera passes that curtain, too, and for a moment the tissue is blown into our faces, as if it was softly floating by just in front of our noses. For Wenders this was a way of exposing the audience to the depth of the film early on.

"A curtain caressing you, almost tickling you, seemed a gentle way to introduce negative space," he says. "I was very aware of the fact that quite a big part of our audience were going to be newcomers to 3D, and I didn't want to shock them. In that scene I wanted to give them the feeling they might grab that curtain or wipe it out of the way."

Other instances include a moment when a dancer blows autumnal leaves toward the audience and again during *Vollmond*, a water-based dance. According to Derobe both are natural situations—you get wet when you are close to splashing water, and when leaves are blown towards you that is how you experience them.

"However, if somebody is pointing a gun at somebody else in the movie and all of a sudden they point it at you in your seat instead, then you become very self-conscious of your role as a viewer. In the case of our leaves the effect brings you closer to the action and involves you, in the case of the gun you become the victim of a premeditated act of the filmmaker, and after a short surprise you are driven out of the story.

Fig. 3.18 Fast lateral moves that were not following a movement on stage were "disastrous."

PINA, Ruth Amarante with dancers of the Ensemble of *Le Sacre du Printemps* © NEUE ROAD MOVIES, photograph by Donata Wenders.

"When there is a reason for it, I have nothing against exiting from the screen plane a bit and coming forward," says Derobe. "But strong immersions really take away from the narrative and kill all identification, involvement, or implication with the story."

Thinking in Space

As filming proceeded Wenders began to think a little differently from the way he had approached direction over his career spanning over 40 movies. He began thinking in terms of three-dimensional space and how it could be used.

"My security blanket has until now been little scribbled drawings for each scene, sort of a shorthand storyboarding, difficult to decipher for anybody else, that I usually prepare the night before. In 3D, these doodled frames didn't help me to imagine the entire space you

Fig. 3.19 The water-based dance *Vollmond*.

PINA, dancers of the Ensemble of *Vollmond* © NEUE ROAD MOVIES, photograph by Donata Wenders.

organize with each shot. Actually, I love that the organization for 3D is less cerebral and much more physical.

"When you are on location, and when you have the set and its space in front of you, you can seize your frame pretty quickly. But somehow, even the term 'frame' is not quite appropriate any more. When you frame something, you define it by definition in a two-dimensional way: by height and width. 3D breaks the frame. It puts things outside of it, to the front and behind. We should start using a different word for that process, not one that is defined by its limits."

He adds: "In a two-dimensional world, it is always 'bad' if something in the background is covered by a foreground object. If two actors are aligned for instance so that the one closer to the camera is blocking the view of the one further back you have to interfere. 'Make sure you see the camera' is what you always tell the people in the background. In 3D that fear of alignment is gone. Actually, sometimes that effect is even good, because

Fig. 3.20 *PINA*, Aleš Čuček © NEUE ROAD MOVIES, photograph by Donata Wenders.

it brings out depth nicely, and you always feel the person in the background, anyway, when you move your head. Like in life."

The real revelation for Wenders during the shoot was his discovery of volume. From watching *U2 3D* he understood the potential of space and depth, but nothing had prepared him for volume.

"I first saw it when one of the dancers (Dominique Mercy) was lying down on a table, and the camera was moving in on him, until his whole body just fit into the frame, seen from a slight low angle and in a perspective that caught his head and his shoulders in the foreground.

"There it was, all of a sudden: the volume of his body. The roundness of his shoulders and its muscles, the sculpture in space that we connect to our regular vision, but that in 110 years of cinema somehow has been eliminated from our perception in film. That body lying on the table had phenomenal 'presence,' for lack of a better word. He was there in the most physical way."

Fig. 3.21 Contrary to the recordings on stage, Wenders had much more freedom in outdoor locations (an industrial refinery, "hanging" metro, quarry, park, and swimming pool) to see the choreography from different sides. Wenders says he chose the locations in relation to their 3D spatial potential and also to help bring out the best of each solo dance performance.

PINA, Anna Wehsarg © NEUE ROAD MOVIES, photograph by Donata Wenders.

Wenders was able to transfer this physicality to the static silent portraits of the dancers, which acted as connecting sequences between the dance performances. Their thoughts are heard narrated over the top of short filmed portraits showing each of them individually sitting in front of the camera, at a distance of about four feet. These were Wenders' favorite moments of the entire shoot.

"They were alone for this shot. The crew left, and I stayed with the camera, but behind the rig, so the dancers could not see me. On a little 3D monitor I saw the unbelievable volume or physicality that each of these portraits had. It seemed to me that for the first time the aura of a person was also translated to their image. This is what finally convinced me that 3D was not just an ideal medium for dance, but also for the documentary of the future. I wasn't sure if stories could handle so much real presence, so much existential being, but I was pretty excited by the idea that future documentarians can base their films on it."

PINA is neither a fictional film nor a conventional documentary. In a way, filming something that is choreographed is akin to shooting something fictional. And of course, documentaries are not devoid of storytelling to begin with.

Fig. 3.22 Thinking in space.

PINA, Robert Sturm, Aleš Čuček, Tsai-Chin Yu, and Wim Wenders © NEUE ROAD MOVIES, photograph by Donata Wenders.

According to Wenders, *PINA* was documentary in the sense of "preserving something that you consider beautiful," so that it can be shared with others. But both realms, fiction and documentary, are still huge white areas on the map of 3D cinema, which he feels filmmakers have barely begun to chart.

"If we agree that 3D is indeed not only a new technology, but also a new film language, it is obvious that it needs its own grammar and its own vocabulary," he states.

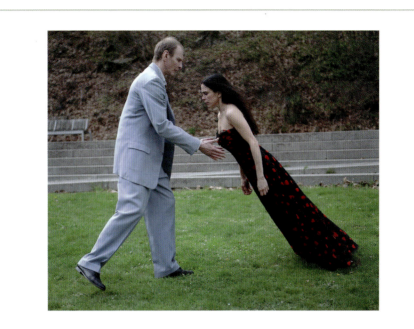

Fig. 3.23 ... the aura of someone that we can almost touch...

PINA, Ruth Amarante and Andrey Berezin © NEUE ROAD MOVIES, photograph by Donata Wenders.

Fig. 3.24 The real revelation for Wenders during the shoot was his discovery of volume.

PINA, Rainer Behr © NEUE ROAD MOVIES, photograph by Donata Wenders.

CARMEN IN 3D

Carmen in 3D uses its additional depth to approximate a theatrical experience within the confines of a cinema. The film is a recording of Georges Bizet's opera as staged by Francesca Zambello at London's Royal Opera House (ROH) over two performances in 2010. It is produced by Phil Streather through his company PLF and directed by Julian Napier.

The co-production between the ROH and 3D cinema specialists RealD is both a record of an opera as well as an attempt to recreate the experience of being at the performance.

While 3D cinema films of ballet had been shot (*Giselle 3D* filmed at St Petersburg's Mariinsky Theatre and *Swan Lake* shot at the ROH) *Carmen*'s director Julian Napier and producer Phil Streather knew that they wanted to take a different approach, which for them, meant placing more cameras on stage.

"I was getting feedback that some test shoots done on opera and ballet had fallen short of the mark, particularly in terms of miniaturization because the cameras had been set at the back of the audience," says Streather. "If you work with long lens shots you can't expect the 3D to look anything other than cardboard."

He explains: "If there is not enough interaxial distance between the lenses in a shot the objects can look flat and cut out. If there is too much then objects can appear miniature and deformed. Instead we want to achieve a natural roundness to the 3D and this ratio of roundness should remain constant and relative to the objects around it."

Streather told his executive producers, "We are going to have to put cranes in with cameras that can reach the other side of the orchestra pit, and please let us get a Steadicam on stage."

With that agreement, Napier began two months of intense storyboarding culminating in the creation of a 90-second 3D animation of one of the *Carmen* arias, which helped to convince RealD and the ROH of the approach.

"The intention was to offer the best seat in the house, but a seat that is continually shifting as we move and find the optimal angle to view the performance from," says Napier. "I certainly wanted to optimize the 3D experience for the viewer but at the same time to disguise it. I believe that the minute you show the mechanics of 3D and make the audience aware of it you are distracting them from the story. You treat 3D as an additional toolset, primarily to tell a narrative.

Figs. 3.25 and 3.26 "Few people have seen opera in the cinema, fewer still have seen 3D opera," says Napier.

Images copyright RealD and Royal Opera House, photographs by Ollie Upton.

"Right from day one on the project I was conscious of walking a very fine line between trying to create a visceral experience for people but not to overstep the mark and contrive something that will pull them back into the cinema and make them realize they are wearing glasses."

Since Napier had only two live performances from which to create the film, a rigorous storyboarding process was crucial to plotting camera positions and moves.

"We wanted to be on stage or very close to it so we were constantly running the risk of one camera moving into another camera's shot," he says. "We had to get the cameras to perform a well choreographed ballet where they constantly yield to one another, moving into close-ups and out again.

"Because we were working multi-camera on a live event there were inevitable compromises. Sometimes you do have to shoot something on a slightly longer focal length than you'd prefer. Although we rehearsed Steadicam moves so the cast could get used to the operator we were not going to be able to stop and retake a scene. I tried to plan everything to give myself as many options as possible, to get as close as possible and to minimize the times when I would be on longer focal lengths."

Napier's camera placement was informed by the mix of large-scale tableau (featuring 100 cast members at times) with the opera's more intimate emotionally charged moments.

"We used wide shots to give a sense of scale and geography and then close-ups for the intimate scenes," says Napier. "With 3D, though, you don't want to jump cut from long to mid to close-up but transition fluidly, letting the camera grow into the close-ups at a pace, in this instance, determined by the arias and by the emotional intensity of the performances.

"I am not conscious of it, but for me the 3D effect of the whole film is like waves breaking along a shore. The 3D works in tandem with the camera movement, into and out of the action, following the oscillation of the drama and the music."

Napier was able to plot the 3D throughout the entire storyboard process. That the 3D was achievable from any one camera position at any one time was integral to making his final shot choices.

Napier opens the film with some glimpses of the cast in their dressing room and behind the curtain, putting the final touches to their preparations in the moments before the

Fig. 3.27 Using a Technocrane enabled a camera move to start from a high angle and move slowly nearer then into the performers on stage.

Image copyright RealD and Royal Opera House, photograph by Ollie Upton.

opera begins. Once the curtain has been raised the large cast is seen filling the stage and he delivers the first of three planned signature moments, which act as a recurring motif throughout the show.

For the first 3D moment, which starts from a high angle on a Technocrane and moves slowly nearer and nearer then into the performers on stage, Napier wanted to present a statement of intent.

"Few people have seen opera in the cinema, fewer still have seen 3D opera, so I wanted to show them what to expect from the experience right up front. It was slightly hyper-stereo but not with overkill," he says.

"There is also real drama in this moment. It is a flash forward and we see a man (Don Jose) condemned to death for killing the woman he loves. He is on his knees holding out the rose that she gave him and the executioner comes and grabs him to take him away.

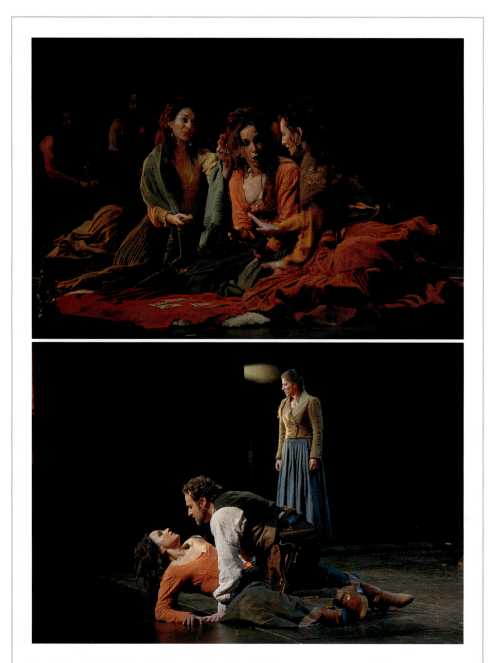

Fig. 3.28 and 3.29 Napier: "The 3D works in tandem with the camera movement... following the oscillation of the drama and the music."

Images copyright RealD and Royal Opera House, photographs by Ollie Upton.

I wanted to start high and end with him in total isolation, in medium close-up (MCU), arms outstretched, exposed in a pool of light. I wanted the audience to see that he has a rose in his hand and for that to emerge out of the screen plane to convey this strong sense of emotional attachment."

"I try and make my use of space very virtual so that if the subject is 30 feet away from us then the convergence point should feel that far away. The scene starts in 1% positive parallax (behind the screen) otherwise we have nowhere to go with the 3D and you risk miniaturization. As we come in closer I want him to emerge from the scene, ending on around 2% negative disparity (in front of the screen) on his hands, so that the audience feels they can take the rose from him."

A similar move was planned for the middle of the opera but was sidelined when it proved logistically impractical, but a shot at the finale mirrors this 3D moment, with the focus again on the rose.

According to Napier working in 3D requires an appreciation of new film grammar as well as some additional vernacular. One of the main ways this manifests itself is in composition.

"We need to be sensitive to the fact that we are presenting our story world in 3D and this is arguably more realistic than 2D simply by virtue of the fact that we are creatures that perceive the world we live in, in three dimensions," he says. "In reality people selectively choose their own close-ups, our eyes are constantly scanning; think about the how often they shift around and perceive possible risks just while driving a few hundred yards down the road. We seem to be far more perceptive and alert to 3D information than we are of 2D.

"So in many ways when you block moves for 3D you are presenting people with a picture of a scene and you can allow the performers, an object, the lighting or shifts in special emphasis to draw people's attention to where you need it, you can reveal a point of interest without necessarily having to use a cutaway or close-up."

Napier adds that when watching 2D our eyes are converged on the screen plane throughout the entire film. In 3D however they constantly have to reconverge on objects set at variable distances from the viewer.

"Reconverging your eyes, like any muscle reflex, requires a duration of time to achieve; our eyes don't just snap into a new position. If you are not sensitive to this basic anatomical truth then you will cause eyestrain and worse nausea. You have to shelve one

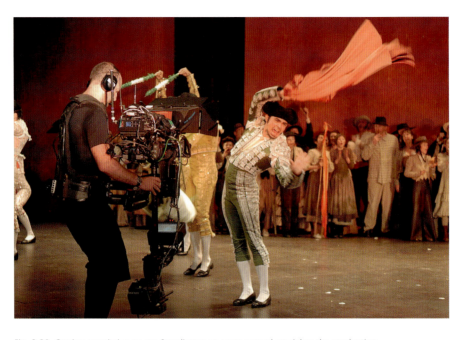

Fig. 3.30 Getting permission to use Steadicams on stage proved crucial to the production.

Image copyright RealD and Royal Opera House, photograph by Ollie Upton.

or two 2D conventions in order to safeguard against this but then every medium has its own peculiarities and limitations. Oil paint doesn't behave the same way as watercolor but in the right hands each can invoke a powerful emotional response. Personally, I'm excited to be working in this emerging medium, one that is constantly revealing new secrets to me."

A follow-up of the opera *Madama Butterfly* was quickly put into production by RealD/RHO, again produced by Streather and directed by Napier, with largely the same crew but with one key operational change.

While *Carmen in 3D* was recorded with the stereo pullers having to converge at theoretical distances in order to place the subjects at the desired point in space, *Madama Butterfly* was recorded with the convergence mostly set on the furthest point of interest in each scene, so that the final convergence/depth placement could be set in post.

"The end result makes for a more stable and consistent stereo placement with a lot less convergence 'hunting,' therefore requiring less attention and correction in post," says Streather.

CIRQUE DU SOLEIL WORLDS APART

Cirque du Soleil describes its own style as "a dramatic mix of circus arts and street entertainment." Artists perform elaborate dances, death-defying balance stunts, acrobatics, physically strenuous movements, and contortionist poses, all dressed in outlandish costumes and makeup. Perfect material then for 3D technology to capture and a project that had fired the imagination of James Cameron when Cirque du Soleil's Executive Producer Jacques Méthé approached the Cameron | Pace Group to take charge of its stereography.

Fig 3.31 Production on Cirque began with multiple cameras and ended up using just four.

© 2011 Cirque du Soleil, photograph by Mark Fellman, costumes by Philippe Guillotel.

"For quite a while we were convinced that it was impossible to put Cirque onto screen in a manner which even approximated the real thing," says Méthé. "A lot of what makes Cirque such a box office draw is simply about being there in front of what is happening at that moment. We'd filmed several Cirque shows in 2D with interesting results but none had ever attained the 'wow' factor that the live experience brings. However, we felt that in the right hands, 3D technology could bring something new to the table. The right hands are clearly someone like James Cameron who understands where to place the camera to achieve the best 3D perhaps better than anyone else."

With the idea of a 3D movie embedded, Cirque's management explored ways of presenting the content. Would they record one complete show from beginning to end or try to arrange a live transmission to cinemas? They decided instead to combine acts from various Cirque du Soleil shows, including Ka, with its climatic battle on a vertical stage, and the water-themed spectacular O, which features an acrobatic act on a ship that floats above the pool of water, linked by a new dramatic story.

Rather than take the logistically challenging route of transporting the 3D production to Cirque shows located around the world, elements from some of the seven shows playing in Las Vegas were chosen. Filming took place over a month in the winter of 2010-11 with Andrew Adamson (director of *Shrek* and *The Chronicles of Narnia: The Lion, the Witch and the Wardrobe*) assigned to write the linking narrative and to direct, Cameron as Executive Producer and Vince Pace overseeing stereo production.

"There were reasons for working with an A-list director," explains Méthé. "We wanted to tell a story linking sequences from different shows. We also felt that the structure of the Cirque shows necessitated a more cinematic approach to filming in 3D than one which simply recorded straight performances.

"For example, a typical rock band will have three static band members and one running around whereas a typical Cirque show has up to 70 performers on stage operating front and back, stage left and stage right, and up and down," says Méthé. "The high levels of life-endangering aerial acrobatics and complex machinery of a Cirque show also make filming a lot more complicated. We have an x-, y-, and z-axis as opposed to a regular rock and roll shoot where nothing much happens at height."

To capture all the action meant breaking the main sequences into their constituent parts and then filming them again and again from different angles before assembly in the edit.

"The initial approach was to shoot with multi-cameras but we soon realized that this was not a good option," says Méthé. "It was difficult to put the camera at the right place and not see another camera in shot. We started with twelve cameras and as we proceeded we narrowed that number down until, when it came to the last part of the shoot, we were using just four cameras. In doing so we went from a shooting style of a rock concert or live sports event to a production style more akin to a movie."

Fig. 3.32 and 3.33 It was vital to get the cameras in the midst of the action to capture the dynamism of the performance.

© 2011 Cirque du Soleil, photographs by Mark Fellman, costumes by Marie-Chantale Vaillancourt.

It also became clear that camera placement was critical, and that cameras positioned where the audience would sit were not viable. For Cameron, who also wielded one of the CPG Fusion 3D systems as lead camera operator, it was vital to get the cameras in the midst of the action and to follow the performers wherever they went (see Fig. 3.32 and 3.33). That meant cameras on booms and Technocranes as well as rigging the operators up to positions alongside that of the performers.

"The performers are in jeopardy the entire time," Cameron said during a presentation of sequences from the film at the 2011 IBC conference. "The 3D camera gets right up there with them, you feel the height when they are performing 90 feet above the floor. You see the amazing physicality of the performance—the strength, the grace, the beauty."

There are some wide and long shots made during public performances but 90 percent of filming was conducted solely for the 3D film, allowing camera operators access to the stage itself. "Because the choreography is so complicated we wanted the cameras to be where they would get the best point of view," says Méthé.

For Méthé, the result is a new piece of art that is not attempting to mimic the live experience of being at a Cirque show but one which will take even seasoned Cirque fans to places they haven't been before.

"We have a narrative piece and the viewer is invited into that world to watch what happens. They are not outside watching it take place in front of them, they are surrounded by the action and the characters," he says. "They are placed right in the middle of it which is a completely different take from bringing you a traditionally filmed show. The stereography gives you a sense of being there that is more acute than any other methods. 3D makes it more exciting, more real and brings you closer to the emotion of the story."

Fig. 3.34 The feature does not attempt to mimic the live experience of being at a Cirque show but attempts to capture something unique.

© 2011 Cirque du Soleil, photograph by Mark Fellman, costumes by Dominique Lemieux.

Author's Note:

As the book went to press, Paramount Pictures acquired worldwide distribution rights to Cirque du Soleil Worlds Away.

REFERENCE

[1]   Alain Derobe sadly passed away in March 2012.

4

LIVE SPORTS: INTO THE ACTION

Live sports are arguably the most difficult of any content to film in 3D. Unlike other live events such as concerts or ballet, the fast movement and random nature of the action can't be rehearsed, although patterns in play can assist planning.

The approach to filming athletic competition is one that is still evolving—and each individual sport requires its own unique approach—but something that those involved at this early stage agree on is its potential to involve audiences in a way far greater than one can with a 2D experience. The extra dimension allows the viewer to feel the height, the distance, or the speed of an event to a greater extent than possible in 2D. A 3D window into the sports world can bring audiences closer to the experience of the event—which in the case of an event as steeped in tradition as the Olympics or Wimbledon, can be as unique as the sporting event itself.

A 3D close-up can also allow the viewer to share an intensely personal and emotional moment with an athlete, such as determination, or anguish. At the highest level of athletic competition, this is indeed powerful.

"3D can extract the core athleticism, character, and emotion from a sport far better than 2D," says Vince Pace, who has completed over 40 live 3D sports broadcasts ranging from the X Games to golf's The Masters Tournament. "The eye-opening moment for me was shooting golf for the first time in 3D where the stereo allowed you to see the undulations of the greens and the true landscape of the course in a way that 2D never can. In that sense 3D elevated the backdrop to a star."

But considerable challenges were evident from the start. Before Sky in the UK began its ambitious sports effort, a weekly English Premier League soccer match delivered to pubs and clubs from April 2010, the broadcaster worried that the only exposure many UK viewers would have had to stereo 3D were theatrical releases, with *Avatar* the benchmark for what the 3D experience meant.

The producers joked that it would be difficult for a soccer match to compete with stereo effects finessed over four years when all they had was four seconds. A concern was that audiences would be underwhelmed by 3D presented on the small screen, which would necessarily be conservative in its use of 3D moments to reduce the risk of errors.

Another worry was that such 3D moments would also have to be minimized so that fans could watch a two-hour match (or longer in sports like five-set tennis) without eye

While it may be technically hazardous, sports are a natural genre for the 3D treatment, permitting fans to experience the atmosphere of an event as if they were there. That at least is how the marketing literature for 3D sports broadcasts might put it. The reality is a little more prosaic.

For reasons of budget and the practicality of working within already tight stadium confines, those involved in early productions spent considerable time testing and developing best practices with some opting to use a 3D crew separate from the 2D production, while others developed formulas that adhered closely to the 2D version using the same broadcast equipment and crew.

"There is no business model that makes any sense for two separate productions," says James Cameron, who formed 3D technology and services supplier Cameron | Pace Group with Vince Pace [1]. "A lot of people are insecure with that idea and want to have the comfort of 2D not being changed in any way and to add 3D separately to that. That is fine—but you can't cry about how much it costs when there are other ways to do it."

ESPN's vice president, strategic business planning, Bryan Burns agrees: "From a business standpoint, we have to get to a point where it makes sense to use 5D (joint 2D and 3D production). Separate productions across the board create a financial situation that is not sustainable [2]."

"There is still a steep learning curve with live 3D sport," believes Peter Angell, HBS Director of Production & Programming. HBS (Host Broadcast Services) is the Swiss-based production company behind the host broadcast for all FIFA events. "Everybody needs to get better and more creative at using 3D from stereographer and cameraman to director. My concern is that the pressure on economics is trying to find a shortcut to an end result that hasn't been fully explored. I'd rather see 3D spend another year or more maturing as a much better 3D product and then look at how integration is best achieved."

All the major sports broadcasters have tried their hand at 3D in all types of major sports from darts and cricket to horse racing and basketball. Angell still believes not enough work has been completed in 3D to develop a standard approach, and that the whole production is still in an experimental phase.

"We need to reach an agreed standard approach to 3D coverage before we look at shortcuts to achieving a combined 2D/3D," he suggests. "The visual language of live 3D sports is not yet developed and too many shortcuts will stunt its growth before it has had a chance to show what it can really do."

A look at the approach to the FIFA World Cup 2010 and Wimbledon 2011 tournament follows, offering some perspective on a variety of challenges, as these were both events that were broadcast around the globe, both for 3DTV audiences as well as for theaters equipped with digital cinema projection and satellite services. Audiences therefore were

Fig. 4.1 Wimbledon 2011 marked the first time 3D cameras were allowed to cover action from the hallowed Centre Court.

Image courtesy Bob Martin / AELTC.

seeing these broadcasts on varied screen sizes and viewing environments—and no doubt brought with them differing expectations.

FIFA WORLD CUP 2010

As the team behind the broadcast of the 2010 FIFA World Cup in 3D found out, 3D gave viewers—and the broadcast's directors—a greater sense of spatial awareness that enabled them to show the match from different angles in a way that 2D could never replicate.

Where a high-profile soccer match will be ringed with 25-32 HD cameras, including all manner of specialist point of view devices to give a very precise "directed" view of the game, they found that a 3D coverage of a World Cup soccer match could pause for longer on shots and provide viewers with the best seat in the stadia to watch the action because the additional spatial information was giving viewers a better understanding of the position that they were watching from.

In covering 25 matches live in 3D over a month the production proved a great logistical achievement that pushed the boundaries of what was possible with existing equipment.

According to one of its technical leads, the Creative Director of CAN Communicate, Duncan Humphreys, "We were trying to achieve a universally accepted level of 3D which would be considered a good experience by audiences who had not been exposed to 3D before."

In the period since the World Cup, the workflow and technology continued to be refined such that by the time the FIFA broadcast participants reteamed for the first 3D broadcast from Wimbledon in June 2011 the concentration was on polishing the production values and not just on making the thing work.

The ambitious production for the FIFA World Cup 2010 was only green-lit by the sport's governing body six months ahead of kickoff on December 1, 2009.

At that time 3D sports production workflow, techniques, and technology were in their infancy. Trials had been conducted on several sports including rugby, (American) football, basketball, tennis, and soccer. HBS experimented with 3D broadcasts when it covered the 2008 IIHF World Championship in Canada and, in April 2009, a French Ligue 1 match between Olympique Lyon and Paris Saint-Germain.

But these were all single events, delivered as experiments to select audiences. Nothing had been attempted on the scale of a high profile live-to-air 25-match run, taking place in

Fig. 4.2 A 3D World Cup would not have happened without Sony's financial backing, according to FIFA. Reproduced courtesy of HBS Group of Companies.

Fig. 4.3 The ambitious 3D production of the FIFA World Cup 2010 smashed the scale of any previous live event. Reproduced courtesy of HBS Group of Companies.

multiple stadiums and cities, scheduled over a month. FIFA delivers the World Cup to an audience of 26 billion cumulative viewers and expects nothing to be left to chance even if only a fraction of that audience would be able to see the 2010 3D coverage.

HBS had been working for at least seven months in anticipation of FIFA's ultimate decision. During that time the professional broadcast division of Sony Corp. had turned to HBS to help it develop a 3D processor, which the manufacturer intended to automate key parts of the 3D production process. Other manufacturers were also looking into the technology, but as an official FIFA sponsor, Sony became a key driver behind FIFA's decision to pioneer a 3D project for 2010, and underwrote the cost of the additional production.

According to FIFA director of TV, Niclas Ericson: "FIFA wants to push technology boundaries and 3D was the prime example in 2010. The project would not have happened at all without Sony being prepared to finance some of it [3]."

A 3D production of the world's premier sports event outside of the Olympics played into Sony's strategy to promote 3D content and ultimately 3DTV displays. For its professional division a close liaison with the production team would enable it to speed development on the MPE-200 processor, which was designed to replace the time-consuming and often inaccurate mechanical alignment performed by motorized rigs on camera lens pairs (a common hazard in 2010, since addressed by advanced stereo image processing software; see also the sidebar "No Two Lenses Are the Same" at the end of this section).

Extensive testing of the processor in tandem with Element Technica Quasar rigs, Sony HDC1500 cameras, and standard Canon HJ lenses began in earnest in February 2010 under the command of HBS' Peter Angell, who assumed the role of FIFA special 3D project leader.

Angell contracted London-based 3D production specialist CAN Communicate to provide further technical expertise and together they devised a test regime for the technology and workflow on a series of nine soccer matches that HBS was producing (in 2D) of Ligue 1 for French operator Orange.

"Essentially we were beta testing the Sony 3D box, working with lab versions, cramming the best part of a year's R&D into six months," says Angell. "Sony were incredibly reactive to the observations we made and we quickly learned together what functionality it needed."

Fig. 4.4 HBS conducted a series of tests on French Ligue 1 soccer matches.

Reproduced courtesy of HBS Group of Companies.

Figs. 4.5 and 4.6 After the first few games, all eight 3D rigs in the stadia could be set up in five hours.

Reproduced courtesy of HBS Group of Companies.

In the meantime Sony outfitted two outside broadcast vehicles (owned by UK firm Telegenic and France's AMP Visual TV) for stereoscopic work and had them air-freighted to South Africa on giant Russian Antonov planes just days ahead of the first game on June 11.

The test phase left HBS confident that the technology and workflow would deliver. What could only be tested live however was the time taken to rig and derig the camera systems. Doing this for multiple games, some of them just a day apart and over a protracted schedule, had not been done before. The concern was that it would take the best part of a day but as the crew got more familiar with the process, they were able to set up all the cameras in under five hours.

"That was a revelation because of the implications it had for wider 3D outside broadcasts," says Angell. "We proved it could be done as efficiently as a 2D operation."

No Two Lenses Are the Same

A key issue that live-action 3D, from sports to feature films, has to contend with stems from the fact that no two sets of glass optics are exactly alike. The slightest inconsistencies in alignment, and distortions and aberrations from lenses, focus,

Fig. 4.7 No two pairs of optical glass are identical.

Image courtesy CAN Communicate.

zooming, lens flare, or spherical reflections can produce discomfort or break the stereo illusion. Some lenses even create subtle anamorphic squeezes.

The problem is particularly acute when zooming. According to 3Ality Technica CEO Steve Schklair, since no two lenses track identically, even a fractional misalignment will lead to uncomfortable 3D viewing. The image will not only deviate around the center of the lens during a zoom (horizontally) but also vertically.

Motorized rigs automated by software have been designed to control the interaxial and convergence parameters and to eliminate pitch, yaw, and roll between cameras. Such motorized rigs also ensure that lens length, focus, iris, and zoom (FIZ) are linked as closely as possible.

For live productions where a reliance on post is not an option, obtaining accurate results at source is critical. It is vital that timecode references are genlocked and computer control is established over zoom, interocular distance, and lens length, while each camera's respective metadata is saved.

New software technologies are being used to calibrate the optical centers of the two lenses throughout the zoom range. After alignment an operator can set the required interocular distance of the rig and software will calculate and correct for any misalignment during production.

Camera Positioning

The tests in France were also vital for planning camera positions and the overall editorial approach. A key criterion was to achieve a quality and consistency that at least matched the production values of the 2D product.

"We knew we couldn't compete in terms of the number of cameras (32) and angles available to the 2D broadcast but we also knew we had to tell the story of the game while delivering an enjoyable 3D experience," explains Angell. "We experimented to see what would work editorially including covering the whole match from a position behind the goal, or making a corner position the master shot. In fact what we found is that the classic way of covering football in 2D is not actually a bad base for 3D."

HBS were also sensitive to taking the audience with them. For the majority of viewers the FIFA World Cup would be a first experience of any stereo 3D, let alone soccer, whose style of coverage has been honed over decades.

"We didn't want to get caught in a situation where we were just offering up a 3D shot because it looked good in 3D and negate our prime responsibility, which is to tell the viewer what has happened," says Angell. "Nor did we want to make the jump too big for viewers brought up on a 2D style, which essentially narrates the match from a Camera One position high, wide, and central to the pitch. Even though that position doesn't provide much depth for a 3D experience we needed to include that shot in order that viewers could follow the game."

The conclusion drawn by the team is that the stereoscopic effect is at its best when presented on wide shots close to the action. Pitchside and behind the goal cameras in particular tend to be the ones delivering the 3D punch where the proximity of the lens to the action can provide a strong sense of depth. Although this played into HBS' decisions on camera placement, constraints of space within the stadia and a simple lack of technology capable of delivering robust 3D feeds from Steadicam or specialized angles limited the available choices.

Eight camera pairs were deployed per game including main camera wide and main camera tight—the traditional Camera One and Two angles but set at a slightly lower position in the stands relative to the 2D positions. The others cameras included goal line left/right on roughly the same height as the main two cameras but looking diagonally across the pitch; cameras to the left and right of the substitute's bench; and one on the six-yard line to the side of the goal. Additional POV cameras such as a Spidercam on overhead wire were converted from 2D to augment coverage.

"We placed the eight rigs where the cameras would provide a maximum amount of coverage with the least amount of infringement from the general paraphernalia of a football match—the main one being the linesman," says Humphreys.

In soccer two linesman run the length of half a soccer pitch on opposite sides and always in line with play. "While the camera to [the] left of the bench was fine, the one to bench right really didn't work because it kept getting the linesman in shot," he says.

"Stereo objects in front of the screen plane are problematic if they intersect the edge of frame, as contradictory depth cues are sent to the viewer. Essentially one cue is saying that the object is in front of the screen and another is saying that the object is behind it.

"To get around this we either had to shoot super wide and include him or super tight and try to exclude him but in reality neither really worked so we decided to move that camera and position it as an extra one behind the goal," he explains.

Fig. 4.8 At Soccer City, Johannesburg, a gantry position towards the right corner flag on the same side of the pitch as the main wide and main close camera. HBS felt it should be as close to the six-yard box as possible and as low as the stadium would allow.

Reproduced courtesy of HBS Group of Companies.

Editorial and Direction

In successive matches during the World Cup HBS were able to hone their editorial approach. A 2D soccer match is habitually cut between Camera One and Camera Two (wide master, tight master), however their high position relative to the action yielded little in the way of depth, they felt, to generate a noticeable difference between 2D and 3D viewing.

In marked contrast to conventional 2D coverage, which relies on Camera One to sweep the field of play from penalty spot to penalty spot and from one side of the pitch, the HBS team realized they had more freedom to swap camera positions.

"We felt that the 3D was giving the viewer a lot more spatial sense of what they are looking at on the pitch and from what position they are looking at the action from," says Angell. "When we realized that we found we could move the camera around with less constraint, including crossing the line to shoot from the reverse side of field. We were selecting the camera more or less according to which quadrant of the field the ball was in but still returning to Camera One to balance the 3D. That yielded a fantastic stereo effect without diminishing the editorial understanding of the game.

"The spatial awareness extended to the directors and camera-ops who, after a few games, began to anticipate where the ball was going to land and to precut to the nearest camera. In 2D the cameras follow the action. In 3D we can preempt it. Cutting a little earlier to the player who is going to receive the ball means you can see what he is doing with his feet and body and the skill he has in receiving the ball.

"Effectively we were moving around to the best seat in the stadia depending on where the action was but so as not to penalize the viewer's appreciation of the match narrative."

For HBS, directing soccer in 3D requires a change in mindset from 2D including on-your-feet planning about camera selection to follow the ball across the pitch.

For example, if the ball is in front of a 3D camera position at one end of the pitch and it is suddenly kicked to the other end of the field the director must work out how to get from the first camera to cover the action at the other end of the field. Do they simply cut from one to the other or bridge the move by using perhaps the Camera One stand position?

"In 2D, if the action is moving from left to right all the camera cuts need to be from the same side of the field to prevent the viewer from getting disoriented," explains Humphreys. "Not so with 3D. With 3D, it is easier for viewers to orient themselves, and there is an increased perception of where the camera is on the field. Shooting 3D allows the production to 'cross the line' more often by allowing cuts to cameras on both sides of the field."

While wider shots from the field level introduce more elements that can add depth to a scene, the crew also found a need to frame the main stadium 3D cameras tighter on game action. However this left the operators facing a delicate balance because if they were too tight on the shot it required more panning, or quick movement, which can introduce motion blur into the picture.

Angell was urging the directors to take a few risks in the early matches to find out what the limits of coverage would be.

"It is difficult for directors and crew who have spent a career learning to cut 2D football to suddenly cut in 3D and it takes a while for them to get the new language into their head," he says. "Even at the World Cup you could see that, for a while, a director had slipped back into 2D mode."

"Over the course of the 25 matches we felt that the 3D experience would be much more rewarding for a viewer if they could watch a match from somewhere it [had] never been broadcast from before. This is the idea of swapping over to cameras on the other side of the pitch, or low down, or wherever the interest from the viewer's point of view was at its greatest.

Fig. 4.9 The International Broadcasting Centre (top). A separate commentary to that of the 2D broadcast was necessary (bottom).

Reproduced courtesy of HBS Group of Companies.

"That was something brand new about football coverage because in 2D that would never work. In 2D you can't continually move up and down the stadia or swap sides or effectively change the viewer's seat in the stadium because in 2D there is no spatial awareness to guide the viewer. In 3D the viewer instantly knew where they were on the field from the cameras we selected. That changed our perception of how different an experience 3D could be to 2D."

Standout shots that brought home the dramatic energy of the 2010 event included one at the finale of the Italy vs. Slovakia match when a Slovakian player ran right past a 3D position arms outraised; a similar moment occurred when Brazilian player Kaka dived forward and toward the screen in a celebration again in front of a 3D position, while in the first game the South African team's opening goal was hammered straight into the roof of the net and toward a 3D goalmouth camera.

"That was a big moment for us," recalls Richard Hingley, one of the production's two stereographers. "We had all this nervous excitement built up over six months towards the opening match and you couldn't have scripted a better moment to showcase 3D than the replays of that goal going into the top corner from 30 yards and seemingly out of the screen."

3D moments such as this that lift the experience beyond that of 2D high definition either happen or they do not. Although HBS gently requested that players choreograph their celebrations in front of select 3D camera positions during future games, in the heat of the action they knew this was asking the impossible.

"When the Brazilian team celebrated Kaka's goal they headed towards a camera that had a camera operator waving Brazilian flags," says Humphreys. "We simply got lucky on that occasion because our 3D position was adjacent."

According to Bruno Hullin, one of the two directors working on the 3D World Cup production, "The secret in 3D is to start wide and zoom while, with the lower-pitch cameras, you need to be very wide and have players in the front of the image. Telling the story of the match is paramount and when relying primarily on cameras that are close to the action, the production team needs to learn new ways to follow the action."

"In 2D, I always cut by looking at the men on the pitch because that tells me what is happening," he explains. "But, when I am on a 3D camera on the pitch, I have to look at the eyes of the players to understand what is happening and where to cut.

"You need to find the spirit of 3D, because there are things that are possible in 3D that cannot be done in 2D," says Hullin. "For example, you can stay with a wide shot in 3D

Fig. 4.10 Mirror rig positioned on the line of the penalty area behind the right-hand goal at pitch level.
Reproduced courtesy of HBS Group of Companies.

while, in 2D, you would force the cut and force the view. But, in 3D, you allow the viewer to choose what they want to look."

This creative philosophy has further implications for cutting. The prevailing wisdom was, and still is to an extent, that 3D requires fewer edits than 2D to give the viewer time to resolve the additional visual information that stereo offers to the human brain.

However there were certain moments during the 2010 World Cup when the 3D direction was cut more times than in the 2D broadcast over the same sequence of play with no adverse consequences.

"It works, and it's actually a better game experience for the 3D viewer provided you observe certain basics," says Angell. "You don't want fast whip pans unless tracking with someone running. You don't want to cut between one panning camera to another and especially not one that's panning in a different direction. You don't want 3D replays that begin on a convergence pull because the audience's eyes will not adjust to the transition. These are all adaptations of conventional technique which no one knew when we first started but which we refined and honed with each World Cup match."

Fig. 4.11 The Bench Left camera mounted on a Sheffield plate, located halfway between the edge of the penalty box and the halfway line on the left-hand side of the pitch. Cameras at pitchside delivered the greatest 3D effect but the production was constrained by available camera positions inside the stadia.

Reproduced courtesy of HBS Group of Companies.

Fig. 4.12 The HBS 3D production team, led by Peter Angell, far right.

Reproduced courtesy of HBS Group of Companies.

World Cup Stereography

Cutting in 3D, particularly live when the results cannot be finessed in post, relies on camera placement and complementary convergence (see the sidebar "Depth-Scripting the Coverage" at the end of this section).

"The point of convergence should be similar, if not identical, from one camera to another in terms of the physical space you are looking into," says Angell. "You don't want to cut from negative parallax (in front of the screen) on a player to a shot of the same player from a different angle in positive parallax (behind the screen)."

The depth budget managed that process. For the FIFA World Cup it also had to accommodate simultaneous distribution to 3DTVs and 475 cinema screens worldwide.

"Since every 3D shot is defined as a percentage of screen width into or out of the screen, the percentage difference will always have more impact on a large screen than on a 46-inch TV," says Angell. "We tried to create two different versions of the 3D for cinema and TV but that didn't work so we devised a depth budget that would deliver an enjoyable experience without jarring the discomfort of either."

Even though 99 percent of the total audience for the tournament was expected to watch in 2D, and within the group of 3D viewers the cinema audience was expected to be significantly larger, the production team wanted to ensure that all the 3D viewers of this pioneering broadcast were satisfied.

Balls booted directly toward a 3D camera would make an obviously stunning 3D shot but decisions needed to be made about what the outer limits of the convergence should be. They settled on a depth budget of 2%-2.5% positive parallax (into the screen) and

0.5%-1% negative parallax (out of the screen). Most of the time the stereo was manipulated within a conservative budget of 0.5%-2%.

At around the same time as CAN and HBS were deliberating, Sky Sports in the UK was conducting its own experiments around 3D soccer matches, alighting on largely the same depth parameters for the launch of Europe's first 3D channel in April 2010 (to sports bars and pubs initially and to the home in October of that year).

"Not every shot has to be a whizz-bang 3D effect. In fact over the two hours of a game this would make for uncomfortable viewing," says Humphreys. "We do though want the odd moment to fly out of the screen but those need handling with care."

With this setup, when a player or object comes towards a camera position the convergence puller must react in a split second to rack convergence dynamically (similar

Fig 4.13 FIFA (whose President is Sepp Blatter—front right) was keen to ensure that the 3D production posed no risk to delivery or presentation of its 2D product.

Reproduced courtesy of HBS Group of Companies.

to focus pulling) through the shot, maintaining the point of interest and stopping short of exceeding the limits set by the stereographer.

"My approach is to keep things at screen plane and just let certain objects or players come into negative space at certain moments when it feels natural—such as when objects or players are coming toward the viewer," says Hingley. "With fast moving sport it is of course very difficult to control the 3D which is why you limit the amount of convergence with a depth budget at the outset and orchestrate this with your convergence pullers so that you are all working as a team."

Hingley feels that a key element in the process is to anticipate when to remove a camera that is going to give a bad 3D experience to a viewer.

"That is the number one decision we have to make. Secondly we have to ensure that there is a very balanced depth or look to the 3D when a director cuts between cameras."

Fig. 4.14 Spain, World Cup winners 2010.

Reproduced courtesy of HBS Group of Companies.

"There is a degree of obsessiveness about staying within a depth budget but if you used a machine you would probably produce a production that was too safe, too conservative and it wouldn't creatively use depth," insists Hingley. "Just as you wouldn't replace the creative skill of a camera operator who is framing a scene in accordance with the context of the action in front of them, so a convergence puller's critical judgement can't be easily replaced. Their skill comes from using their own eyes to judge whether the vision is comfortable."

Adds Angell: "Once you've set the depth budget the really interesting thing is to know when you are breaking it. It is fine to break it—you just need to do so for the right reason and you can't leave it to chance."

Humphreys agrees that convergence should be seen as a creative tool in the same way that focus pulling is a creative tool. "If you are doing shading, framing the camera, offering up graphics or replays those are creative decisions. The whole outside broadcast is a creative decision and we've added a creative layer in 3D, although the language for working with this is still evolving outside of specific crews with live 3D experience."

Depth-Scripting the Coverage

A production team is responsible for managing the overall 3D design and supervising the depth balance across all the cameras.

Sometimes the production is depth-scripted. This is a way of planning the parameters of the 3D which for example could mean delivering a greater 3D punch in the first five minutes or to alternate the 3D effect with the ebb and flow of play. In the case of the FIFA World Cup the stereographer played a key role in imparting that information to the convergence pullers, who are able to view the image difference (foreground and background separations) from their stereo pair on monochromatic displays overlaid with a grid. According to Richard Hingley, one of the stereographers, the grid lines afford them an easy way of controlling the crucial interaxial and convergence by altering the parameters of the camera's FIZ (focus, iris, and zoom).

The overall amount of 3D depth into (positive) and out of (negative) the screen is translated into percentages, where 100% is the maximum amount of parallax in either direction. The percentages may seem tiny (0.5% being the amount at which depth was pulled toward the viewer during the World Cup) but the effect can be great and anything more extreme than this can cause eyestrain if performed over an extended period and without due care taken in balancing the convergence across all cameras.

Fig. 4.15 Stereographer Richard Hingley at work in the 3D outside broadcast of Wimbledon 2011. Image courtesy Sony.

WIMBLEDON 2011

Spooling forward a year to summer 2011, the teams from CAN Communicate and Sony worked with the BBC to produce an in-venue 3D experience from Wimbledon's Centre Court on the Championship's 125th anniversary.

"There is no iconic brand like this in the sporting calendar," says CAN Communicate business development director Chris Dyer. "It was a fantastic platform for 3D and it was available. When we approached the AELTC (All England Lawn Tennis Club) all the light bulbs went on."

The basic technology and workflow used in the World Cup was retained and the overseer of the proven FIFA model, HBS director Peter Angell, was signed as executive prouducer.

"We knew the technology worked and that it had been improved in every layer from lenses to cameras to fibre convertors to the MPE-200," says CAN Communicate's

Fig. 4.16 The men's final captured in 3D at Wimbledon 2011.

Image courtesy Thomas Lovelock / AELTC.

Fig. 4.17 Tennis has predictable patterns of play allowing the 3D team to judge in tests where players would be at particular points in a match from the courtside cameras.

Image courtesy CAN Communicate.

Fig. 4.18 and 4.19 Above and below: Test shoots were conducted before and during the two week tournament.

Image courtesy CAN Communicate.

Courtesy Sony.

Duncan Humphreys. "We knew how to record 3D and how to work with it. We'd proved it in South Africa. What was great about Wimbledon was the chance to concentrate on and refine production standards and to really deliver to viewers an experience of having the best seat on [the] court."

Tennis is accepted as far more suited to 3D broadcast than soccer. The tight geography of the courts (particularly at Wimbledon, which is tighter than the French Open's Roland Garros) produce low, close to-the-action diagonals, which are ideal for replicating 3D depth on a small screen.

The audience is closer as well, framing strong depth cues for a TV audience, while the action itself is far more predictable. A player will always serve or receive from a certain point, they will always return to their chairs at certain points. These more calculable actions make the job of the convergence pullers and director much easier because they can predict what is going to happen.

Fig. 4.20 A 3D 'wow' moment as the racquet pops the screen plane.

Image courtesy Bob Martin / AELTC.

The Wimbledon 3D Production

The use of 3D for broadcasting tennis, due to the proximity to the action, seems to permit a greater appreciation for the speed of the top-ranked players and how fast the ball is moving and spinning as they compete.

"Seeing the speed, curve, and trajectory of the ball is not possible in 2D but with 3D you are learning more about the game, gaining an immediacy and sense of position about how the players move and a genuine feeling of what it may be like to be courtside," says Humphreys.

As with World Cup soccer the Wimbledon production team called for longer duration shots and replays, with generally fewer cuts. Ideally, the shots are composed to include foreground and background layers to provide layers of depth while the camera operators are directed to frame wider to avoid forcing cuts and to avoid lateral movement and zooming.

The kit setup and editorial formula approximated that used by CAN, HBS, and Sony during the World Cup including a similar stereo alignment of 0.5% negative disparity (out of the screen) and 2.5% positive disparity for the majority of shots. Likewise, the simultaneous distribution to 250 cinemas meant a more cautious approach than were it for TV alone.

"We couldn't be as aggressive out of the screen as we would like," notes Mark Grinyer, who led Sony's technical team. "That said, when a ball comes towards the screen we let that happen as a one-off event. If we were just delivering to TV we would dial up the wick a little by pushing to 2%-3% from the screen for short periods of time."

Humphreys describes the ideal creative use of stereo for any 3D sports coverage as having the regular rhythm of breathing.

"You don't want to be pushing 3D out of the screen all of the time but to use the 3D gently so that the viewing experience remains natural," he says. "The creative use of stereo is slowly becoming more integrated into the production process in the same way that graphics and replays and other techniques are already integrated and used judiciously to tell the story of the match."

The sport's more predictable nature meant convergence operators could judge with accuracy where players would be at a particular distance from the courtside 3D cameras.

"As a result very little convergence was pulled during the matches," says Humphreys. "Instead we set convergence at a certain level and simply let the players move away and towards the camera, breathing the convergence in and out accordingly since if you were sitting in that position that is what you would perceive.

"In one instance Novak Djokovic reaches for a ball and at that moment the racquet just pops out of screen. That's because we'd rehearsed it enough to leave the convergence point there. It's a 3D 'wow' moment but it feels a natural part of the story of that game point.

The Wimbledon 2011 3D coverage was produced by a separate team with its own cameras, outside broadcast units, and production crew. The unit also had access to specific 2D camera feeds provided by the BBC for conversion into 3D.

"2D/3D conversion in some form or other is going to be needed whether stereo purists like it or not," suggests Humphreys. "Unless the 3D production offers similar production values to the 2D production then 3D will only ever be niche. We chose to work with

Fig. 4.21 Close-up 3D can enhance the emotional intensity of performance.

Image courtesy Bob Martin / AELTC.

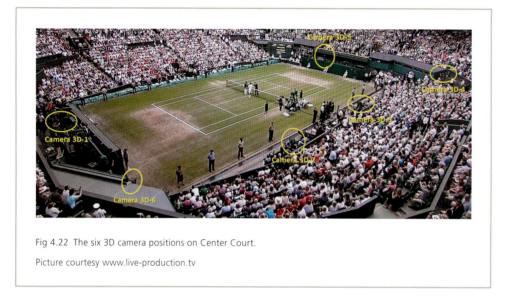

Fig 4.22 The six 3D camera positions on Center Court.

Picture courtesy www.live-production.tv

2D/3D converters [which translate the 2D images into stereo images in real time] in the hope that we can raise the quality of what we deliver. A converted image allows us to tell the story in as complete a manner as possible."

As with the World Cup there were constraints on the six 3D camera positions caused by the sheer lack of space for additional cameras in such a small arena. This will remain the case while 3D is considered secondary to the main 2D operation—or until the two productions merge.

Six camera positions covered Centre Court (all Sony HDC-P1 bodies mounted on Element Technica rigs). Camera One was positioned at the north end on a platform looking over a wall toward the court and much closer and lower than its 2D equivalent with the camera operator directed to frame wide to contain the players and to avoid panning. The position was mirrored by Camera Five directly opposite, which became the production's master camera.

Cameras Two and Three were positioned on the west side of the court on either side of the umpire. A fourth camera was located at the radio commentary position at the southwest corner of the court. A sixth camera caught beauty shots of the crowd.

"We were probably one or two cameras short to cover all eventualities on the court," he says. "One issue was that we had to cover our master camera from the opposite end to the BBC camera position because our 3D rig was just in line of sight for guests in the

Fig. 4.23 The 3D production of the Women's final.

Image courtesy www.live-production.tv

Royal Box. We would also have liked to raise our courtside camera six inches to see over the net and a bit of the baseline, which is something we will aim for next time."

3D outside broadcasts have come a long way since 2008 when CAN and the BBC transmitted its first live 3D HD coverage to a handful of cinemas of an England vs. Scotland rugby match.

"Then, we were lucky to get anything at all," says Humphreys. "That was all about whether we could actually get pictures. By 2010 it was about building a technical production stream for multiple 3D events and by Wimbledon it was a full outside broadcast. The technology is proven, and while there will be technological developments, from here on in much more of the focus is on refining the editorial."

THE ECONOMICS OF DUAL PRODUCTION

HBS' 3D workflow pioneered in 2010 is unlikely to change for the next World Cup in Brazil in 2014, according to Angell. The basic camera positions won't change either although

Fig. 4.24 and 4.25 The intention is to being the audience closer to the action by framing strong depth cues.

Images courtesy Matthias Hangst / AELTC

it's also likely that FIFA will negotiate additional positions lower down the stadia than for its 2D cameras. Additional 3D point of view cameras such as one placed on a crane for aerials, in the goalmouth, or on a Steadicam for roving touchline action are also likely to be introduced giving the HBS team more alternatives to cover each quadrant of the pitch.

The biggest change is likely to be a greater integration of 3D with the 2D production though to what extent is yet to be determined. While there are technical synergies that can brought into play, for example sharing of some camera positions and tighter links between production resources, which technologies for greater control over convergence and alignment will facilitate, the way that soccer is currently presented to viewers in 2D and in 3D are so different that editorial compromise is not yet likely. However strategies vary from sport to sport.

"A 2D and 3D joint editorial works better for some sports than others," says Angell. "Boxing, tennis, basketball for example can be cut together in a way that works for both formats but the editorial is necessarily different between 2D and 3D in (soccer)."

In fact soccer may be among the hardest sports to cover in 3D. The cameras have to cover a large arena and the action is both fast and random. In similar team sports such as rugby or American football the game is far more predictable with set patterns of movement and stoppages for scrums or plays, which allow time for a director and operators to get their cameras into position. The set patterns of movement on more enclosed spaces such as tennis or basketball courts or boxing rings allow for easier stereographic planning.

The experience in the United States of Vince Pace, who has worked extensively for ESPN, CBS, and others on dozens of live sports events including the 2010 The Masters golf and 2010 and 2011 US Open Tennis Championship, leads him to think that it is economically and editorially possible to shoot every sport in simultaneous 2D/3D.

Pace finds that often the standard 2D shot is the optimal one for 3D. "On tennis, for example, we initially rejected the close-up of the head and shoulders of a player that 2D favors, and framed for a wider shot on the player for 3D to see the swing of the racquet," he says. "But after a while we decided to match the 2D exactly and it worked perfectly. The reason was that 2D was going for the reaction shots, which is critical to a viewer's understanding of the flow of the game regardless of the format you are watching in. The 2D shot conveyed the emotion on the player's face, it connected with the audience, in a way which works in 3D just as well if not better than 2D."

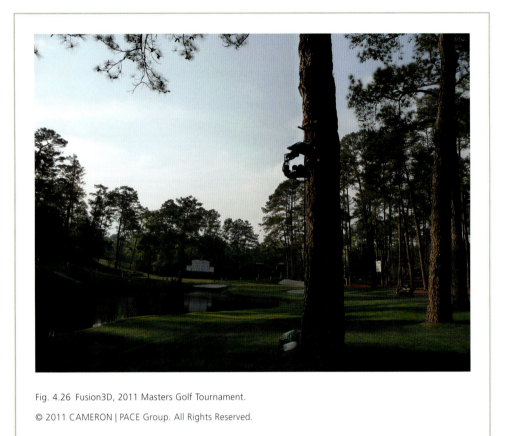

Fig. 4.26 Fusion3D, 2011 Masters Golf Tournament.

Pace's company won a Sports Emmy with CBS Sports for the 2D/3D production of the 2010 US Open Tennis Championship. "I used to say that 3D is the best seat in the house," he says. "But I now realize that the person sitting in the best seat in the house is the 2D camera guy and the 2D director. That's how it has been planned so we have to find ways of working with that, not against it.

"The technology feels like it is restricting the 3D editorial vision at this point—that you can't move cameras fast, that you have to frame differently in 3D, that the high-up angle is flat," he argues. "When you are dealing with tools at a basic level it pushes you into an interpretation of 3D that is unfair. This is what happens when you don't have the right tools to experiment with. The technology should be working with the subject matter, not against it."

Fig. 4.27 Fusion3D FlyCam, Summer X Games 17.

Pace believes that sports production will transition to a "5D" product—that is, one set up producing 2D and 3D feeds. The Cameron | Pace Group, which Pace co-chairs with James Cameron, advocates mirroring all existing 2D camera positions primarily to take the financial burden of a separate production, such as extraneous crew and equipment, out of the equation. CPG's Shadow system piggybacks the 2D camera with two discrete feeds extracted further down the chain.

"The key is camera balance," says Pace. "If you have continuity in stereo you will have continuity in 3D storytelling so that when cutting between 8 or18 cameras you are aware of how all the cameras complement each other."

ESPN 3D has already produced a vast variety of sports in "5D." Boxing, basketball, football, Little League World Series, and many different X Games events have been successfully produced in a joint 2D-3D approach using CPG technology such that costs are almost down to the point where a network can shoot in 5D for the cost of 2D.

Fig. 4.28 Integrated 2D/3D ShadowCam system (side mount) for the 2011 US Open Tennis Championships in 3D.

"A well thought out 5D production can and does meet all the quality requirements of a 2D and 3D show," says Phil Orlins, coordinating producer, ESPN 3D. "As 3D technology continues to improve and offer us more options in terms of cameras, lenses, virtual graphics and so forth the 5D concept becomes easier and more efficient to produce.

Each sport requires an analysis of the production philosophy, he says. "Some sports, like boxing and most X Games events, require almost no philosophical adjustment because the way they are shot in 2D (close to the action) is already conducive to a great 3D experience. Other sports, such as football, that rely on some distant shots with long telephoto lenses may necessitate the use of occasional 2D cameras to get the viewer close to the subject when the cameras are far away.

"Philosophically our goal is to create the best possible visual experience for the viewer," Orlins adds. "3D is an unprecedented leap forward in accomplishing that goal. Sometimes, however, a tight shot of a face from 500 feet away is essential to the viewing experience and a 2D camera with a large telephoto lens is the best tool to create that experience."

A lynchpin of ESPN 3D since the channel's 2010 launch has been the X Games, a dynamic action-packed event that is shot from relatively close proximity and which translates to a great 3D experience. "It takes place on uneven or three-dimensional terrain which truly comes to life in ways never before experienced when it is shot in 3D," says Orlins. "It's a significant technical challenge in that it's a multi-venue event that requires multiple trucks and nearly every flavor of specialty cameras from Ultra Slo Motion to Cable Cams to all types of robotics and cranes. From a philosophical standpoint it translates easily to 3D and we shoot it very much the way we shoot it in 2D."

There is a great deal of harmony between the two views of 3D sports producers. Both see the urgency in reducing the cost of production and the benefit of having new software automate more of the convergence processes. It is on soccer, the world's most popular and commercially valuable sport, that the debate really hinges.

Over time the overlap of 2D and 3D production may be far greater than it is today. Certainly as the adoption of 3DTV sets continues and as audiences become more and more accustomed to live 3D sport the novelty of its presence will reduce. It is arguable that, just as we all accept high definition for granted today, that depth in the picture will also become casually accepted in the mainstream and eventually become the most-watched format.

REFERENCES

[1] There is no business model that makes sense... Cameron was speaking at IBC, September 2011.

[2] Bryan Burns was speaking at CES, January 2012.

[3] Niclas Ericson was interviewed by A. Pennington for *The IBC Daily*, p47, September 2011.

5

DOCUMENTARIES: REAL WORLD IMMERSION

As the first 3DTV channels came on stream in 2010, stereo production was extended beyond feature films. The documentary genre—already used in IMAX theaters—began to gain new interest as programming for the small screen, and within that the subgenre of natural history, proved most immediately applicable.

Science (space) and nature subjects (from the Antarctic to the Atlantic Ocean) have long been a staple for IMAX screens where larger than life environments seemed to benefit from larger than life audio-visual presentation.

On TV, natural history documentaries have always appealed since they promise to reveal an understanding of landscapes and geographies, and a view of human and animal life that is impractical or impossible for most people to visit or get close to.

3D then would seem a natural fit, offering the armchair traveler an enhanced glimpse at reality, intensifying the feeling of "being there." In its clichéd form it can bring the Serengeti or the Amazon a little further into the living room, but in that sense it might follow the same trajectory of technological advance that has delivered us a better quality televisual view of the world from analog black and white to digital high definition.

The shift to 3D adds a layer of hyper-reality to the already sharp HD pictures, enabling an even closer approximation to the natural world, if we believe that adding depth, albeit an illusion of depth, mimics our real-world perception.

However, is it misleading to suggest that 3D factual programming should replicate real life when the amount of depth it is possible to display on screen is a fraction of what we really perceive?

"People talk about 3D replicating real life but I don't think the use of 3D in features or documentaries is any more about recreating realism than 2D is," notes Chris Parks, who has stereographed factual projects including *TT3D: Closer to the Edge*, which takes viewers to the Isle of Man TT motorcycle race; and *Kingdom of Plants 3D*, Sir David Attenborough's look at plant life that is filmed at London's Kew Gardens and produced by the UK's Atlantic Productions for Sky 3D. "Sometimes we are trying to give a realistic feel for the world, sometimes it is a distortion of that reality and sometimes we make it deliberately unreal in order to get a story or point across.

"The strength of 3D in natural history is its ability to explain a subject—particularly subjects we have little experience of," he feels. "If we see a lion we have a fair understanding of what it is and how it moves but when you see insects or plants on a microscopic level for example, or extinct creatures then 3D can open these worlds up."

It may simply be, as stereo consultant Phil Streather observes, that 3D works best on subjects we have little knowledge of because our sense of size and scale hasn't been tuned in to how they should look and feel. Getting the right stereo feel for elephants on the savannah requires a more naturalistic touch because we think we know how they should appear in the landscape. Producers working with dinosaurs on the other hand perhaps have more freedom to play with the stereoscopic sense of scale.

Parks cites an example: film he has stereographed of a chicken's egg in which the camera can see through the semitransparent layers—the membranes, blood vessels, and albumin through to the body of the embryo with the heart inside with blood cells pumping within it. Because it is all separated out in 3D, all the different elements are clear and discrete in a way that would not be possible in 2D.

The same is applicable to the use of macro time-lapse photography to capture plant life. Time-lapse is a traditional natural history filmmaking technique but in the view of revered broadcaster and naturalist Sir David Attenborough in 3D the effects are "transcendent" [1].

Many of the 3D time-lapse sequences in *Kingdom of Plants 3D* have been composed in postproduction using elements from live action, studio-lit sets, and on-location stills photography to build a layered image which shows tiny movements of leaves or insects in relation to each other—an effect the filmmakers say would have been impossible in 2D.

This use of 3D as an educative tool and for showing us something new is used to tremendous effect in *Flying Monsters 3D* where even shots of fossilized rock comes to life with a texture and geometry.

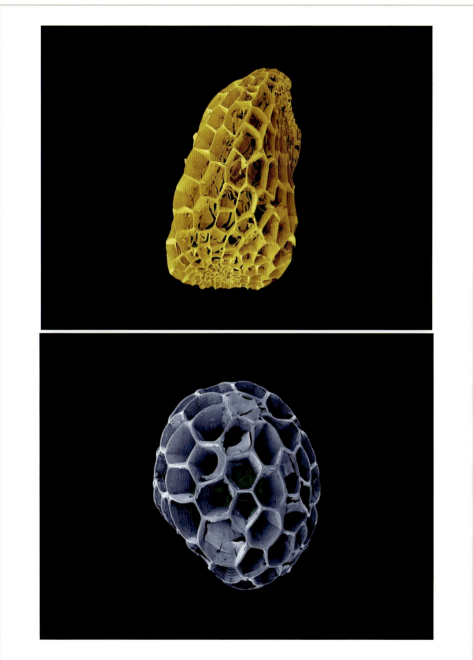

Figs. 5.1 and Fig. 5.2 3D time-lapse sequences in *Kingdom of Plants 3D*.

©Atlantic Productions, photographed by Wolfgang Stuppy.

Whereas that project cleverly worked with inanimate, and therefore completely controllable and storyboarded creatures, *Meerkats 3D,* from Oxford Scientific Films and Principal Large Format for Sky 3D, is an example of a more traditional wildlife doc where the filmmaking approach has had to be flexible to accommodate animal behavior.

"You can play with putting characters or objects along the z-axis as a storytelling device to emphasize changes in story arc on tightly scripted projects but if you do that on observational documentaries you will get into trouble editing," notes Streather. Nonetheless the 3D can be planned to an extent, as Streather outlines in the case study.

The prevailing view is that a conservative approach to 3DTV, where the effects are subtle and the stereo unpronounced, will deliver the most comfortable viewing experience. The fear, at least initially, was that gimmicky stereo effects would cause eye fatigue and kill the format stone dead. There has since been a slight relaxation of that approach to meet the expectations of 3DTV viewers who want something a little different for their money.

"Increasingly we are being asked [by broadcasters] to 'pull' the information slightly more toward the viewer and in more instances," says David Pounds, Chief Executive of Electric Sky Productions. "3D broadcasters need to make an offering to the viewer that is sufficiently different from the experience they would get from HD."

Sky 3D's guidelines, for example, state that negative disparity should not exceed −1% for the majority of shots but includes scope for up to 2.5% out of screen disparity for specific editorial need. As a guideline rather than rule this out-of-screen shot could be extended further if Sky agreed.

"It means selecting the right moments when the subject matter can be angled slightly more toward the viewer," says Pounds. "This poses more of a challenge to the filmmaker because you don't want to overemphasize at the risk of making an uncomfortable experience yet there are certain aspects in every story that if done well and in the right way can be pushed."

According to stereographer Adam Sculthorp, "We actually want the viewer to be engrossed by the 3D in a documentary project in a way that could be considered distracting with almost any other genre. That means we can have a lot of fun with it."

One example is to use hypostereo (using interocular distances smaller than the human average of 2.5 inches) on smaller creatures to bring them larger than life on the screen or to reduce the size of larger creatures relative to the massive landscape they live in.

One rough guide to frequency is that large 3D moments might happen every 30 seconds in theme park attraction films, every three minutes in an IMAX 3D film of 40 minutes duration and about every 12 minutes in an hour-long TV show.

"At times one can explicitly have fun with the stereo—but I would still say that it is important to be intelligent in how we use it," says Parks. "On *Flying Monsters* we used much stronger stereo on the CG elements, bringing the flying creatures out of the screen or putting a lot of depth into the scene when a fossil reformed into its living skeleton. In other sections I felt it was important that the audience wasn't distracted by the stereo.

"If a director wants to use 3D for particular impact on one scene I might ensure there is a less strenuous period leading up so that the contrast in style amplifies the experience in the same way that you might contrast dark and light scenes, saturated with dull colors, or loud with quiet passages. It is about pace and balance and being very aware of the effect that your decisions are having on the audience."

If 3D has the ability to make a subject genuinely immersive then to achieve this you need to be creative in how you use the depth budget, advises Caroline Hawkins, producer

Fig. 5.3 Since the CGI could be controlled many of the stronger 3D elements in *Flying Monsters* were created in postproduction.

©Atlantic Productions / Zoo.

of *Meerkats 3D*. "I'm not a huge fan of the almost entirely positive parallax approach. It's too conservative. Viewers don't expect the 3D experience to be like looking into an aquarium, they want to experience things in negative space too.

Regardless of the style of 3D the central message emphasized over and over again by TV producers and commissioning editors is the need to marry the right story and right subject with appropriate 3D. The core skills of storytelling, including a strong soundtrack and script, should not be neglected in the service of 3D. 3D is no substitute for a good story.

Currently the economics of 3DTV production has many producers looking to maximize sales by distribution to different formats—on one extreme IMAX Dome, at the other perhaps reformatted for iPad™. To keep costs down by avoiding complete reversioning and two separate productions, that usually requires a compromise on the amount of stereo that can be used. What may work as a 3D moment on the small screen could bend the eyes of a cinema audience.

A 2D camera is often taken by documentary crews on location, wielded by a dedicated camera operator to obtain cutaways, reverse angles, and mid-shots, which are helpful in building a 2D edit. Additionally many broadcasters will allow a certain percentage of non-natively shot 3D acquisition (post-converted to 3D), aware that this will keep costs down. Sky, for example, maintains this at 25 percent of a finished program.

Anthony Geffen, CEO and Creative Director at Atlantic Productions and Creative Director of Colossus Productions, suggests that the technical and budgetary restrictions on 3D have meant his team has become better 2D filmmakers. "We've been forced to think about controlling a shot from one place and finding that one good angle," he says. "There is a slight tendency with 2D to shoot several different angles and then slice it together in the cutting room. In 3D you don't have that luxury so you have to be much smarter about how you choose your angles, set up your shots, and tell your story. That makes you a better 2D filmmaker."

The critically acclaimed wildlife documentary team of Vicky Stone and Mark Deeble, who shot a pilot film in Kenya in 2010, also believe in a sophisticated approach to 3D productions.

"As soon as the audience is aware of a shot—which could be a focus pull or sound effect as much as a 3D effect—then their immersion in the story is broken," says Stone. "3D needs to be woven into the story much more coherently than it is now, in sympathy with the story being told. We are still grappling with technology. It is far from being as easy to set up and shoot as with 2D, which must be the ideal. Nonetheless the time has come for filmmakers to move on from stereo basics and to adapt 3D to the creative demands of the story."

Adds Deeble: "3D is a deep-focus aesthetic. It puts the viewer in the scene for longer, so they have the opportunity to look around and appreciate things and explore. It's almost like seeing things through a child's eyes again."

Lighter weight camcorders and recording equipment is being advanced to enable a more fleet of foot operation and to overcome early handicaps in filming observational and wildlife docs in 3D.

"I am convinced that 3D is the future of documentary filmmaking," says Wim Wenders, whose documentaries include *PINA* and *Buena Vista Social Club*. "In a very short time 3D technology will be available and affordable to documentary producers. Then, their films will be able to transport audiences in a very different way into the lives and the work spaces of their subjects. We will be able to share unknown worlds in a very physical, immediate way."

FLYING MONSTERS 3D

Atlantic Productions' *Flying Monsters*, commissioned by Sky, is claimed by its producers as the first film intended for exhibition on an array of formats spanning IMAX 2D and 3D, IMAX Dome, 2D and 3D cinema release, and TV. It is also claimed to be the first time an IMAX film has had an on-screen presenter (Sir David Attenborough) and was one of the first 3D documentaries intended for general cinema release. It became the first 3D program to win a BAFTA (for Best Specialist Factual in 2011).

It carried a small feature film budget, rare for hour-long TV documentary projects, and leaned heavily on computer graphics to tell the story of prehistoric pterosaurs. The show's success boils down to a strong storytelling concept in which 3D proves an ideal explanatory medium.

"In 2009 we were working with Sir David Attenborough (on the 2011 Emmy Award-winning BBC series *First Life*) and pondering future projects together when 3D came up in conversation," explains producer Anthony Geffen. "We discussed what sort of subjects would benefit from stereo and also what was technically possible."

Baring in mind that at this point there were very few 3D content reference points for Geffen to draw on—mostly IMAX documentaries or feature animation—and the process of planning, shooting, managing, and postproducing stereo work was an experiment for all involved.

Fig. 5.4 Sir David Attenborough at the sea bird sanctuary Bass Rock.

© Atlantic Productions.

However Attenborough immediately recognized the opportunities and limitations that the technology might lend to natural history filming. In a career spanning 50 years, one of the world's most respected broadcasters was no stranger to technology, having helped pioneer 16mm for TV documentaries in the 1960s and, later, shot groundbreaking wildlife series in color and using infrared cameras.

"The technology is limiting although the results can be liberating," Attenborough says. "That's why you have to choose you subjects carefully to exploit the full value of 3D. We chose to work with fossils because they can be animated and therefore the 3D can be controlled. I deliberately chose that of a creature which moved in three dimensions so that we could demonstrate its 40-foot wingspan to an audience in a way that conventional techniques could not."

3D is literally used here to bring the subjects to life, a conclusion the BBC came to when commissioning its first recorded, CGI-intensive 3D projects *Planet Dinosaur* and the feature *Walking with Dinosaurs 3D*. It's no coincidence that *Cave of Forgotten Dreams* and *Fields of Valor: The Civil War* (both featured below) are evocations of the past that their producers felt could best be told in 3D.

The combination of strong subject matter and the lure of the iconic Attenborough as narrator convinced Sky that this was the flagship project it needed to headline the Christmas 2010 schedule of its new 3D channel. Atlantic now had less than a year to realize it.

"Since this was such an important project for Sky we knew we needed it to show off what 3D could do and that meant playing with different techniques," says Geffen. "The most extensive element was photorealistic CGI, which allowed us to recreate a prehistoric environment and control the 3D. *Avatar* came out around the same time as the commission (December 2009) and while that had taken several years and a multi-million dollar budget to create we had just a few months. We knew that if our graphics were not to a high level we would fail."

Stereographer Chris Parks describes the approach to the stereo design. "We were looking for the 3D to add to the audience's understanding of the subject and to get them involved in a similar way that you might use a rousing score to make an audience feel excited about select moments.

"At the same time it was important not to distract from what the director (Matt Dyas) was trying to communicate. With that in mind we set out to keep the 3D quite relaxed when David is talking to camera, in a similar way to how you might use softer lighting when shooting a portrait."

Attenborough was placed slightly further back in the shot than they might otherwise have done so that the audience could concentrate on what he is saying, rather than worrying about the mechanics. "When we move into visuals that show what they describe we had a bit more fun with the 3D," adds Parks.

That sense of fun is clear throughout the program. Its creators brainstormed ways to tell the story, discarding ideas that didn't forward the narrative or impart information in ways that didn't showcase what the stereo could do.

This included close-up shots of the fossils themselves in which strong use is made of depth to help explain an otherwise relatively flat subject. Another example is of a short scene filmed at seaside town Lyme Regis. It describes how amateur paleontologist Mary Anning made some of the first pterosaur discoveries. Her story is in part recreated in the painting style of the 1800s, depicting the scene in 3D as it may have looked in that period.

"3D can tap into parts of the brain that 2D cannot since more of the brain's depth perception is used in stereoscopy," says Parks. "3D is particularly effective for tapping memories and with this moment I wanted to try and draw on memories of seaside visits."

"When we began thinking about the story as a 3D production it felt very restrictive and we were conscious of all the things we couldn't do," says Geffen. "Then we realized we had to approach it in a different way. I told the team to forget everything they had learned in 2D. We storyboarded every shot specifying every shot size and angle and found that we had to throw away a lot of our 2D mindset to make the most of 3D in every shot."

For most of the audience, seeing anything in 3D was and remains a novelty. Parks was aware he needed to help the audience relax into the experience so that the effect was an enhancement, not a distraction—and certainly not a substitute for a strong narrative.

On two occasions, one with a backdrop in London's Natural History Museum and another in a laboratory, Attenborough is joined on screen by an animated fossil or animated computer diagram. The first instance literally brings an inanimate set of bones

Figs. 5.5-5.7 Sir David Attenborough studies Mary Anning's Dimorphodon fossil, found in 1829, as it comes to life through computer animation, in the Natural History Museum.

© Atlantic Productions / Zoo.

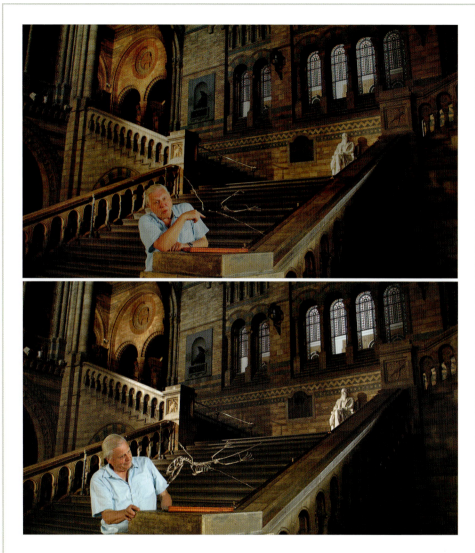

Figs. 5.5-5.7 Attenborough is joined on screen by an animated fossil.

to life, fusing them into a recognizable small flying creature. In the second instance a wire frame computer simulation emerges from a computer screen and walks and flies around a lab, interacting with Attenborough, to illustrate a particular point about its movement.

Both sequences benefit from being created in 3D and would not have had the same educational impact in 2D.

"We wanted to use the stereo to help explain the geometry of fossils that over millennia under rock have become distorted," says Parks. "The use of 3D and animation helps make sense of how the bones were arranged to make up a skeleton."

The sandstone facades of the NHU and the moody, soft lighting arranged by DP Tim Cragg provide a subtle and dark backdrop, which enabled Parks to pull the 3D more into the foreground. The wire frame sequence is in a modern science-fiction style lab with big plasma screens and high-tech instrumentation. In that context, says Parks, it made sense to treat the 3D differently. The scene also has a sense of fun with some fairly rapid cuts as the creature is followed hanging off walls and a hat stand with the stereo drawn "lighter and more gently."

Later, 3D is used to enhance the drama of the monster flying alongside Attenborough in a glider. CG shots of the pterosaur are composited against background plates of clouds, while the glider with Attenborough in its cockpit was shot from a helicopter. This was cut with further shots of Attenborough in the glider speaking to the camera.

Figs. 5.8-5.10 A CG model was created to show how a long-tailed Pterosaur might have moved.

© Atlantic Productions / Zoo.

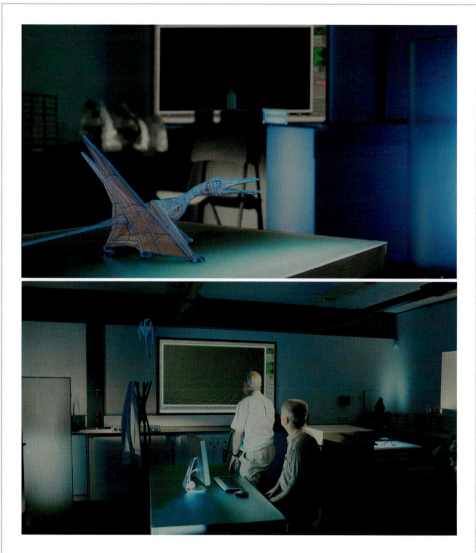

Figs. 5.8-5.10 The sequence continued.

"For the CGI scenes where we had close control over the depth, we pulled more out into theater space to give the audience an impression of flying with the creatures and to impart a sense of scale," says Parks. "If you play the 3D too strong, though, creatures of this scale can appear miniature and toy-like."

Figs. 5.11-5.14 Mixing animation with live action, the production was entirely previsualized.

© Atlantic Productions / Zoo.

Figs. 5.11-5.14 140 shots needed CGI or other elements integrating into live-action backgrounds.

Of the 340 shots in the final program, 140 were either CG, stills, or post-converted elements that needed integrating into live-action background shots in New Mexico, France, Germany, and the Eden Project. Atlantic's VFX subsidiary Zoo handled most of the CGI with some animation outsourced to other companies.

The multiple deliverables presented the production with some huge challenges, not least having to frame each shot and design the 3D so it worked on both a 100-foot IMAX screen and a domestic TV—without the luxury of multiple takes.

To cope with the different formats, a pair of Red One cameras was selected for production. The producers felt these would deliver sufficiently high resolution when blown up to the largest screens, yet not look degraded by the necessary loss of resolution when resizing the frame for TV screens.

"Because wider angle lenses give the best and most engaging 3D we used those even on close-ups rather than switching to longer focal lengths," explains Parks. "Being forced to work in a more considered way did constrain shooting a little but it actually worked well since we were trying to achieve a focus on the information and the narration rather than on lots of cuts."

Capturing to IMAX Dome was particularly extreme with Parks and Cragg mindful that the image would lose the corners of the frame on projection. "If you frame a standard full shot for TV it's likely that the presenter's head will be behind you when projected on IMAX Dome," explains Parks. "To compensate you need to keep the primary subject framed a third to halfway up the screen and take close-ups much wider than you normally would for TV."

The production was also mindful of creating a program that would stand up to scrutiny in the archive. "Currently the quality threshold for 3DTV stereo is generally low," says Parks. "Audiences aren't used to seeing 3D so they accept this but if they look back on it in 10 years time the effect could look awfully dated and the errors really standout. Since a Sir David Attenborough documentary is timeless we wanted to create a high quality product that you could replay in a decade and not notice the joins."

The success of *Flying Monsters* scrambled Sky into commissioning a further raft of projects from Atlantic with whom they partnered to form the 3D focused production house Colossus Productions.

First up was *The Bachelor King*, a narrative documentary about a penguin colony on the island of South Georgia, a subject again of Attenborough's conception in part because of the dramatic landscape, and in part because the crew could get in amongst them and film.

"The thing about 150,000 penguins on a beach is that they look identical so that when they move or you lose track of them during filming you can construct the story from

Figs. 5.15-5.17 Atlantic Productions aimed to create high quality computer animation on a fraction of that film's budget.

© Atlantic Productions / Zoo.

Figs. 5.15-5.17 Several sequences in the CGI scenes were pulled into theatre space.

another one quite simply," Attenborough says. "The other beach inhabitants included seals, and they don't move too fast either."

Penguins are creatures of habit and the judicious choice of subject meant that individual and group behavior could be predicted with some degree of certainty by a team of scientists prior to scripting.

"We were in the right places enough of the time to get some very detailed behavior on film including tiny nuances of movement which are very expressive," says Geffen, who posted a 17-strong crew to the island for six months, typically carrying the 560 kg camera rig onto the island (where camping was banned) and over very tough terrain each day.

"We storyboarded the entire shoot simply because every time you move equipment across ice you have to know the shot you are going for. We weren't trying to make a blue chip natural history doc like *The Blue Planet* but trying to make a very specific story.

Fig. 5.18 Filming Elephant Seals at Gold Harbour, South Georgia for *The Bachelor King*.

© Atlantic Productions, photographed by Oskar Ström.

"It may be that the whole way we make documentaries, and wildlife docs in particular, changes when you shoot 3D. The camera and rigs are too cumbersome and too expensive for a crew to be sitting there for weeks and weeks on end trying to capture singular moments of animal behavior, while run-and-gun style shooting with handheld 3D camcorders is also currently impractical."

A strong subject and a strong story it seems remain the keys to 3DTV docs. For its third project Atlantic chose to build a three-part series around the *Kingdom of Plants 3D* at Kew Gardens using macrophotography.

"In each case we are using 3D to show something very different, each with a strong story, each pushing the technology further forward," says Geffen. "It is very rare in broadcast to use the same equipment as used in big budget feature film productions but we [are] using similar rigs, cameras, postproduction tools, and stereography teams. The real creativity in 3D is in the TV documentary business.

"We don't have $100m budgets so we have to innovate," he elaborates. "We are commissioned by broadcasters with 3D channels who demand that the audience be delivered a sufficiently different experience for them to subscribe to their services or invest in 3DTVs. The economic imperative to make 3D good on TV helps push TV producers to play with the medium."

MEERKATS 3D

According to Phil Streather, CEO of Principal Large Format and producer of the 2003 IMAX film *Bugs! 3D*, the ideal wildlife subjects are either large enough and slow enough to get relatively close up to (say, elephants) or small enough to get almost 100% control over (as with *Bugs! 3D,* which used macrophotography to show insect life in the Borneo jungle).

The subjects of Oxford Scientific Films 60-minute TV production *Meerkats 3D* (in association with Principal Large Format), for National Geographic Channel and Sky 3D, ticked the box of being relatively small; and the production was additionally helped by the fact that a group of the animals in South Africa's Kalahari desert were habituated to human presence. Part of a research establishment based in the Kalahari, the group had been used in previous documentaries featuring meerkats, but never in 3D.

"Meerkat family structure has many parallels to our own structures and the groups we were filming had been studied for so long that the researchers were able to understand which was the dominant male or female, [and] which were their pups and help us as filmmakers to then build a narrative arc around that family," explains Caroline Hawkins, the project's producer. "This group had been studied by researchers at Cambridge University led by Professor Tim Clutton-Brock over a 15-year period enabling the filmmakers to look at the scientifically documented life history of any given animal and see how it related to others in the group."

Explains Phil Streather, the meerkat project's 3D producer and lead stereographer, "Once you have found a great subject the 3D then works best when you achieve a natural volume or roundness to objects. To achieve that roundness you have to get relatively close and film with a wide-angle lens. Filming objects at a significant distance and zooming into them requires a pretty large interaxial distance (distance between the centers of the lenses) to get an acceptable level of roundness; often too great for producing comfortable 3D.

Fig. 5.19 The production team didn't seek an overt 'in your lap' experience' but enough to psychologically change a viewer's relationship with the subject.

Photograph by Andrew Graham-Brown courtesy of OSF & NGC.

"Another way of putting that is that if you have a small enough interaxial to make the 3D comfortable, when using long lenses, then the 3D can end up looking like a kiddies pop-up book or a series of cardboard cutouts."

Streather dislikes a conservative approach to stereo design, which typically places the object of interest at the screen plane. "The orthodox approach is to place objects on or behind the screen plane but I believe that the great unexplored zone of 3D storytelling is the 0.5%-1% negative parallax of objects coming off the screen," he argues.

"That is not the same as poking people in the eye with gimmicky 3D but it also means not being so conservative that you miss the impact that negative parallax can bring. If you take care not to make the 3D come out of the screen consciously, then the audience won't think that their space is being invaded.

Fig. 5.20 Streather (kneeling) with Humble setting convergence parameters ahead of the African shoot.
Photograph by Andrew Graham-Brown courtesy of OSF & NGC.

"Negative space is there to be creatively tapped," he insists. "TV is not simply a window to another world. I liken it more to an open window without glass which permits objects to emerge from the screen, naturally.

"If a meerkat is 2 feet in front of the camera and I am sitting 8-9 feet in front of the screen and the TV is 2.5 feet high then there is every reason that the meerkat should be emerging through that window toward me. I actually think that creating stereo in this way draws less attention to the physical frame of the TV set and with a 0.5%-1% negative you add a feeling of presence. It is not an overt 'in my lap experience' but enough to psychologically change your relationship with the subject."

With all the planning in the world it is near impossible with observational wildlife documentaries to know how the shots captured on location will be cut together. This means that the stereography at the point of capture has to be consistent, to enable a smoother editing process.

"We were using the same 'characters' to maintain integrity (rather than substituting one meerkat for another) but shooting over ten weeks and perhaps intercutting sequences

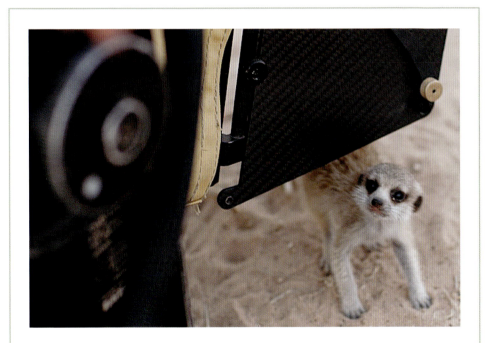

Fig. 5.21 Stereography at the point of capture had to be consistent.

Photograph by Andrew Graham-Brown courtesy of OSF & NGC.

from week 3 with week 9, which immediately reduces the scope for a very strict depth script," explains Streather.

"We planned one 3D moment where we wanted to push the negative parallax—which is when we introduced a trained cobra into the meerkat's habitat—as it happened that has ended up being one of the more conservative shots in the film. Even trained animals don't necessarily do what you want them to do. The rest of the piece was designed to give as much sense of presence and a feeling of being there as possible," he adds.

Essentially that meant that when a meerkat appeared as a certain size in the frame, the filmmakers knew what degree of negative or positive parallax it should have.

On a trial run at a wildlife park in the UK and then on location in South Africa, Streather programmed a chart for the first time location stereographer, Ralston Humble, containing calculations for multiple scenarios of focal lengths and distances to the closest subject. The results of these choices could then be discussed with the film's director Andrew Graham-Brown and director of photography Robin Cox at the end of each shooting day, watching the 3D rushes on a 46-inch 3DTV.

"With the camera at any given distance from the meerkat, with a particular distance from the background and knowledge of the focal length from the DP, Ralston would be able to look at the chart (assuming the sun was blinding him from looking at his 3D monitor) and set an appropriate interaxial for that shot, which would stay within the overall 3% depth budget I had prescribed for the film," explains Streather. "On the flip side of that, when the meerkat filled a certain size in the frame then Ralston could check the chart and note what the interaxial should be set at. That sounds like making 3D by numbers and to an extent it was, but in a constructed and thought through way."

This approach was not slavishly adhered to. By referring to the chart during the day's shoot then watching the footage in the evening the team knew that if they liked what they saw in the rushes they were on the right track.

"This was easier shooting for TV rather than IMAX since viewing on a 46-inch 3DTV is pretty much the target screen size," says Streather. "If there was too much or too little 3D in the shot they could adapt their modus operandi. The whole process worked just beautifully."

Focal Lengths

Traditionally, wildlife filmmaking has relied on using long focal lengths to zoom in close to subjects and achieve a shallow depth of field, but that style is almost the

Fig. 5.22 One of the few planned "3D moments" involved a cobra.

Photograph by Andrew Graham-Brown courtesy of OSF & NGC.

antithesis of "good 3D" in which the foreground and background are more distinctly separated.

"That is not to say longer lenses can't be used at all and there are a number of tricks that can make them work in your favor," says Streather. "For instance, by trying to get the object you are filming close to solid backgrounds. Then you can increase the interaxial (the distance between the two lenses) to increase roundness, without creating too much parallax in the on-screen background.

"In *Meerkats 3D* we have a significant number of shots at 60mm focal length on a 2/3" sensor, which you might think would result in unnatural looking cardboard cutouts," he explains. "We found that if we raised the camera up and looked down on our subjects, so that the main background feature was sand in and around the meerkat burrows, we could still get good roundness. This was because the distance between the meerkats in the frame and the background was short enough for us to increase the interaxial to introduce naturalistic roundness without having an uncomfortable level of background parallax."

This technique works especially in natural history because we don't have an intimate understanding of the scale and shape of wild animals and their environments. It works less well when shooting people.

"If, when shooting people, you pull the lenses too far apart then you can introduce miniaturization, an effect which we are very sensitive to," says Streather. "Humans are of course objects we precisely know the size of, so it's far harder to trick the brain if the scales are not right. But we don't intuitively know how tall a tree is or how big that tree is in relation to an animal for example.

Fig. 5.23 In the Kalahari reserve: Andrew Graham-Brown, Ralston Humble, and Robin Cox.

Photograph by Andrew Graham-Brown courtesy of OSF & NGC.

"One of the myths of 3D is that you need an infinite depth of field to have a good 3D shot. There are so many rules that if you are not careful you can restrict yourself and miss out on all sorts of good shots. For macro shots you can have the background completely out of focus but it shouldn't matter that you that can't see detail in the background because your attention is focused on the glorious detail of the close-up insect or plant. But, if you use shallow DOF, make sure the closest objects are in focus because the human brain is more comfortable not seeing focus in the background than it is not seeing focus in the closest subjects in the frame."

Julian Thomas, Director, *Secret Life of the Rainforest (3D)*

Julian Thomas has shot in the Panamanian rainforest for the 60-minute show *Secret Life of the Rainforest* (produced by Electric Sky Productions for Sky 3D and Smithsonian) as well as in Kenya and Tanzania for *Wildebeest Migration*, an Electric Sky Productions documentary for 3net.

"Shooting in the rainforest is one of the best setups for 3D because there is so much variety in the depth of shot from foreground subjects to distance objects, with larger subject creatures like monkeys and macro close-ups," explains Thomas. "It is also one of the hardest environments since it's very easy to get rain splash or humidity on one lens, not another, or on the mirror. Lens flare is an issue under the dappled light of the canopy and there are always insects that might land on one lens. For this reason, in Africa we mounted the mirror and therefore one of the cameras upside-down, to minimize dust hitting the lens. All of these practical issues just make it harder to do 3D than 2D.

"Ultimately you are still telling a story and you can't simply shoot something in 3D and just expect the story to stand up. The storytelling and the technology should be keyed to the same goal. So, for example, you can use 3D to bring out the emotion and feeling for a story in a way that you can't do in 2D by creative use of the z-axis. Narrowing the interaxial (the distance between the stereo lenses) from a camera positioned at the top of a tree canopy creates a sense of vertigo, whereas widening the interaxial in the undergrowth would induce a more claustrophobic feel.

"Another example: If your subject is a lion and you want to emphasize the viewer's sense of threat you might want to keep the convergence point behind the lion so that when it moves it seems to 'jump' through the screen plane. On the other hand if you are telling the story of a female lion looking after her cubs you may chose to maintain convergence with her so she feels less of a predator.

"In a 3D shot your eyes can do the work that an edit would normally do for you. Instead of being directed where to look by an editor's cut decisions, a 3D viewer should be allowed to take more time to absorb the greater information in a shot.

"For example, if your subjects are insects on the bark of a tree, in 2D you would start wide, frame closer, and then do another CU on the insects. In 3D you can hold that first shot longer and let your eyes wander around the image and effectively let the audience edit the film.

"However, I also believe you can dissolve the convergence points at the transitions between successive shots so that you create a smooth migration of convergence position rather than it jumping with every cut. If you don't do this, your eyes would work like windscreen washers and that would hurt."

Fig. 5.24 *Secret Life of the Rainforest (3D)* used both a large P1 rig with Kerner mount, and a much smaller SI2K rig with prime lenses, for macro and action shots.

© Electric Sky Productions.

Fig. 5.25 *Wildebeest Migration* was primarily shot with Sony P1 cameras from the top of a Land Rover. The cameras were fixed onto a Chapman plate and arm, to absorb vibrations as the vehicle traveled. The whole unit weighed a metric ton, and had to be mounted on reinforced bars welded onto the chassis of the Land Rover.

© Electric Sky Productions.

CAVE OF FORGOTTEN DREAMS

Among the most challenging conditions of any stereo 3D project to date, Werner Herzog's *Cave of Forgotten Dreams* was shot largely in a cave, occasionally using the flickering image of a flame from a Macbook to mimic conditions 35,000 years ago.

The feature documentary, Herzog's follow-up to his Oscar-nominated *Encounters at the End of the World*, was commissioned as a conventional 2D shoot by The History Channel's production wing History Films and UK broadcaster Channel 4, with Herzog only taking the decision to shoot in stereo a week before filming began in April 2010.

Herzog initially resisted shooting in 3D until he saw the caves. He told *The Los Angeles Times* that at that point he realized 3D was the perfect tool "to capture the intentions of the painters" [2].

The Chauvet Cave in the Ardèche, southern France, was discovered in 1994 and contains hundreds of cave paintings depicting at least thirteen different species, including horses, lions, panthers, rhinos, and hyenas. The artists used charcoal to draw on the contoured surfaces in techniques not often seen in other cave art, making it a priceless record of Paleolithic life.

"There's one place where there are lions painted on the side of a rock outcrop, but positioned as if hiding and ready to pounce on rhino, which are painted on another wall," explains Phil Fairclough, former executive VP of development and production at producer Creative Differences. "The artist has clearly used the topology of the cave to tell the story and filming it in 3D would show the artist's intention."

Fig. 5.26 The 3D cameras were custom-built for the production, and were often assembled inside the cave itself.

Photo by Marc Valesalla. © MMX Creative Differences Productions, Inc.

Access to the cave has been extremely restricted due to concerns that overexposure, even to human breath, could damage the priceless drawings. By agreeing to use lights that emit no heat Herzog was the first filmmaker to succeed in gaining permission to create a feature-length film inside the cave. For The History Channel this rare opportunity could scarcely be passed up and a 3D shoot would be a valuable archive document.

At the time of production in early 2010, 3D documentary technology and technique was rudimentary. Techniques for 3D filmmaking in natural environments with a single camera and no compositing were largely undeveloped, and had to be worked out experimentally by the crew in postproduction. Moreover the French government's understandably tight filming restrictions meant separate shoots for 2D and 3D were out of the question. The producers were only handed a short window of six days in which to film.

For the director of such uncompromising work as *Aguirre: The Wrath of God* and *Fitzcarraldo*, taking technology to its limits in the pursuit of a vision was second nature.

"The technology choices were largely determined by what could we get our hands on and also what was sufficiently mobile and lightweight to be assembled and then function in a very cramped environment," says Fairclough. "We ended up using the four-day reconnoitre, which would normally act as a test period, as part of a ten-day production schedule to maximize the time available."

The caves have 99% humidity and high levels of carbon dioxide and radon making it impossible to work inside for more than a few hours a day. Further restrictions meant only four crew were allowed inside the cave at any time—Herzog, cinematographer Peter Zeitlinger, stereographer Kaspar Callas, and a sound recordist or lighting cameraman.

Filming was permitted only from the narrow metal catwalks that span the cave and to guard against damage to the walls; the rigs had to be dismantled, carried, and rebuilt inside the cave for each session.

The producers sought technical assistance from specialist underwater and natural history cameraman Dave Blackham and camera designer Jonathan Watts. For the opening sequence of the film, to set the scene for the cave's external location in the landscape, Herzog wanted an aerial shot. A six-rotor helicopter designed by Watts was configured for 3D aerial shots with a pair of $300 GoPro HD Digital cameras velcroed onboard.

Another innovation was the use of an animated flame on a laptop to provide the sort of flickering firelight that would have made the paintings themselves seem animated in prehistoric times.

Figs. 5.27 and Fig. 5.28 The crew was allowed to use only battery-powered equipment they could carry into the cave themselves. Herzog worked the lights himself. The crew could not touch any part of the cave's wall or floor, and were confined to a two-foot-wide walkway.

Photos by Marc Valesalla. © MMX Creative Differences Productions, Inc.

Fig. 5.29 Herzog believed 3D was the only way to capture the original artist's intentions.

Photo by Marc Valesalla. © MMX Creative Differences Productions, Inc.

Fig. 5.30 Peter Zeitlinger and Werner Herzog on location.

Photo by Marc Valesalla. © MMX Creative Differences Productions, Inc.

Launched in early 2011, 3net is a 24/7 3D network in the US and a joint venture of Sony Corporation, Discovery Communications, and IMAX Corporation. The channel has already used 3D to take viewers on journeys, including across Africa, America's National Parks, and into the world of bullfighting.

One of its most ambitious productions is the four-part *Fields of Valor: The Civil War*, which combines 3D live reenactments with remarkable stereoscopic stills photography from the 1860s.

"Our original idea with the Civil War was to see if we could produce history in 3D," says Tom Cosgrove, president and CEO of 3net. "In the course of research we discovered that there is a large reserve of 3D photographs from the time of the Civil War. We thought, 'Could we build a story around it?'"

The 3net team tracked down thousands of stereoscopes from this period, which were provided by the United States' Library of Congress. Stereo stills cameras would record two versions of a scene onto separate cards for viewing through a stereoscope. The popularity of this art form only waned with the arrival of moving pictures at the turn of the century.

"These photographs take our understanding of the era to a whole other level," says Tim Pastore, who executive produced. "Most people have never seen these photos. You see the battlefield come to life—here is a real battlefield and a real casualty of war."

"(For instance, there are images) of guys who are out on the No Man's Land, sitting there just waiting, as if they were snipers. Those photos in 2D don't raise a lot of emotion, but in 3D it puts you right there."

To forward the story, the production team additionally lensed scripted reenactments and added a narrative from actors who portray actual soldiers in the Union's 20th Massachusetts and the Confederate's 1st Virginia regiments.

"There are a lot scenes where the characters are talking directly to the camera, and they are carrying the story as the character they are playing," Cosgrove says. "The 3D makes that experience even more intimate. You feel a little closer, as if they are in a room talking directly to you.

Cosgrove adds that 3D was also used for emphasis, an example being a shot where a female slave is whipped. The woman is in the foreground and the man who is doing the

Fig. 5.31 3net built its production on digitally restored stereoscopes and native 3D dramatic reenactments.
Library of Congress, Prints & Photographs Division, Civil War Photographs.

whipping is in the background. "This is about the emotion of what she is going through, he is less important. She is in the foreground; your eye tends to go to what is most negative in the shot. That tells the viewer emotionally where to respond."

The other element of the production involved bringing the battles to the living room. "A lot of times we were building depth into the screen, bringing the landscape and the battlefield to life," Pastore says. "We used wide shots to try to convey the landscape

Fig. 5.32 Reenactments were shot in 3D.

Fields Of Valor: The Civil War / 3net.

of the country and the scope of certain battles. One of the largest battle reenactments was recreated to look as if it involved 40,000 people. We shot over a couple months in multiple locations, from Illinois to Virginia using actors and battle reenactors. Director David Padrusch was able to run the entire gamut from handheld all the way to those vista shots as well as smaller POV rigs for some shots to put the viewer in the midst of the action."

Fig. 5.33 Library of Congress, Prints & Photographs Division, Civil War Photographs.

Fig. 5.34 Fields Of Valor: The Civil War / 3net.

REFERENCES

[1] Sir David Attenborough in interview with A. Pennington, p8, *IBC Executive Daily,* September 2011.

[2] Is Werner Herzog's new 3-D documentary a huge forward leap or total folly? By P. Goldstein and James Rainey, *Los Angeles Times,* September 13, 2010. (http://latimesblogs.latimes.com/the_big_picture/2010/09/is-werner-herzogs-new-3d-documentary-a-huge-forward-leap-or-total-folly.html)

6

DRAMA: A CLOSER CONNECTION

More than any other film, *Avatar* has shaped and continues to shape audience perception about what 3D means. James Cameron's 2009 sci-fi epic produced by Lightstorm Entertainment and distributed by 20th Century Fox—for many viewers, their first look at live action digital 3D—went on to gross more than $2.8 billion at the global box office and scoop many accolades including Oscars for visual effects, cinematography, and art direction.

Avatar's producer, Jon Landau, describes 3D as creating a "sensory experience," which is no more apparent than in the psychedelic design of *Avatar*'s world Pandora and in the film's action-packed battle sequences.

For Laudau however, among the most compelling moments in *Avatar* are the more intimate dramatic sequences rather than the action scenes. He highlights the moment where Neytiri (*Avatar*'s heroine) throws Jake (the hero) out of the Na'vi spiritual home, Hometree. "Because the 3D puts the audience in the Hometree with the rest of her clan, all of a sudden I feel like a member of the clan emotionally involved in watching it happen."

Visual effects supervisor Joe Letteri explains: "Up to this point we had lowered the interocular distance a little in scenes featuring Jake and Neytiri so it feels more intimate between them. But in this scene, we started to open up the stereo a little more, so when you are looking at Jake from Neytiri's point of view, the world feels a little bit bigger and you feel this distance between them. In 2D, you are aware of the gap between them, but in 3D you can now feel how far they are apart emotionally."

Landau further describes 3D as an "almost voyeuristic experience" enabling audiences to connect with the intimacy of shared moments between characters.

Since *Avatar*, a growing number of filmmakers such as Peter Jackson (*The Hobbit*), Ang Lee (*The Life of Pi*), Ridley Scott (*Prometheus*), Martin Scorsese (*Hugo*), and Baz Luhrmann (*The Great Gatsby*) have explored how stereoscopy can enhance a story's dramatic potential, by using the third dimension as an element of the narrative.

At its most basic stereo can enhance a story's dramatic potential by making a visceral connection with an audience. An emotional depth, if you will. An example of this is given by Buzz Hays, Senior vp, 3D production, Sony Pictures Technologies. He describes a scene in *The Silence of the Lambs*, when Clarice Starling and the audience are first introduced to Hannibal Lecter.

"Director Jonathan Demme has both characters standing apart, separated by the glass of the prison cage. Then as Lecter steps toward her he cuts to a close-up and you see the performance in [Anthony Hopkins'] eyes, which almost makes the hair on the back of your neck stand up," says Hays. "In 3D, if you treat the exact same situation in a different way but instead of cutting to a close-up, you have him take a step into your personal space, it is now a physical reaction.

"By making Lecter come out of the screen into negative parallax you engage the audience in a way that speaks to the whole basic human instinct, which is to regard this character invading your personal space as a threat. That is the power of the language of 3D storytelling. We are starting to establish grammar to help make this language make sense to people."

Hays welcomed both Ridley Scott and Baz Luhrmann to Sony's 3D Technology Center, in preparation for their own first forays into 3D where they explored the relationship between the stereo camera and actors, particularly in intimate story moments.

The ability to work with actors in three-dimensional space is theatrical. If, in a theater performance, an actor can achieve a direct emotional connection with the audience that is lost when rendered in 2D, could stereo 3D bridge the gap and bring performance and character closer?

Some of the most effective 3D moments in *PINA*, for example, don't focus on dance at all but occur in the interludes when each of the dancers relates a memory of their mentor, Pina Bausch, straight to camera. Wenders explains that instead of setting the convergence point at or behind the screen plane, which would have made the subject appear further away and the effect more observational, the subject is drawn toward the audience in order to create an intensely personal connection.

With these shots Wenders describes seeing for the first time what he calls the "aura" of a person translated along with their image.

"The sheer presence of a person in front of us, the aura of someone that we can almost touch, the roundness and physicality of a body," he says.

INTIMACY IN *AVATAR*

The action sequences in *Avatar*, in particular the climactic battle sequence involving hundreds of dragon-like creatures (Ikran) and super-tech military hardware is extraordinary, but the impact of those scenes would be lessened without the film's emotional heart.

"The world of Pandora is a character in its own right," says Landau. "When the audience is taken with Jake into Pandora for the first time [on helicopter, away from the military base] you are meant to feel as if you are flying into the rainforest on that flight into a new world that you are so intrigued to discover." The thrilling feeling of movement in space gives the audience an opportunity to share in the experience of the characters.

When wisp-like floating creatures called Woodsprites slowly land on and then envelop Jake, it is as if they are recognizing the spiritual connection Jake has with Pandora's nature, even if he himself does not. At this moment the sprites appear in front of the screen as if to surround the audience.

Says Landau: "When Jake glances up and we follow his gaze we—and he—see a Woodsprite coming down and it feels like it is within our touching distance in front of the screen before it floats back to Jake. The 3D emerges from the screen plane only because it is at one with the narrative. It doesn't take you out of the moment."

Letteri says that generally speaking they kept convergence at screen plane, focused on the eyes of the characters. "That is the easiest way for the audience to follow action sequences the whole way through," he says. "It is also the most realistic way to convey the drama of intimate conversations since in the real world our eyes converge around the eyes, or very near to the eye of the person we are speaking to."

The aesthetic use of 3D should broadly mirror that of human vision, agrees Landau. "Human eyes have to do two things in synchronicity with each other. They converge on an object of interest and focus on that object. As humans, we cannot separate out those two functions. In my opinion the best philosophy when creating 3D is to converge on our subject of focus so when it is projected in the theatre the subject of focus appears as if it is at the screen plane. By converging on a subject in focus we can cut between shots as quickly as we want because the audience eyes are always converging in one spot and their eyes are not jumping back and forth between convergence points."

Figs. 6.1 and Fig. 6.2 Filmmakers including Ridley Scott and Baz Luhrmann have workshopped stereo shoots at the Sony 3D Technology Center, a training facility whose partners include the International Cinematographers Guild, the Directors Guild of America, and the Motion Pictures Editor's Guild.

"I think what makes *Avatar* successful is not any one element—the 3D, or the sound, or the production design. I think it is how all of those things are worked together. The scene when Jake first meets Neytiri is a great example of that. The pink flowering objects in the background are defining the set; the Woodsprites are coming down (and immersing the audience); while the music (composed by James Horner) resonates with the normal touchstones of a big Hollywood orchestral score, at the same time as it feels tribal, as if it is part of the indigenous culture of Pandora. All these elements are combined to complement and enhance the love story between our main characters."

THE CLOSE-UP

The close-up is arguably the most powerful dramatic shot. And numerous filmmakers interviewed for this book believe that 3D can make such a shot all the more impactful.

"2D is a flat photographic interpretation of three dimensions because depth and angles are only implied," says visual effects supervisor Rob Legato. "2D naturally flattens out the features of an actor's face. So if 3D gives back some of those angles then it is more truthful to an actor's performance. That, of course, depends on the performance but since film acting is by nature more subtle than theater acting—where the actor must project their emotion—the nuances of a good screen actor's performance can be shown more clearly."

As to the performance itself, actor Andy Serkis (Gollum, *The Lord of the Rings*; Captain Haddock, *The Adventures of Tintin*) notes that the actor need not "act" any differently.

"I don't think 3D makes any difference as an actor. You are just in the moment," he says, while observing that "[The close-up] continues to be the way into the soul of a character."

Director Eric Brevig agrees: "The director should be getting the best performance regardless of the format they are shooting in," but he notes, "because the viewer has twice the visual information (in a 3D image) it will be much clearer, in any intimate scene, to see what's going on."

Stereographer Simon Sieverts, who has studied the psychology of stereopsis, argues that if done properly in 3D, the close-up can reveal the emotional state of a character far better than a 2D version.

"Evolution has made us into experts at judging others based on facial expression," he contends. "Scientific tests suggest that facial expressions based on real emotions tend to be symmetric, meaning both sides of the face are similar.

However, he says, our perception of facial symmetry is hindered by our own physiognomy, in which human vision is only accurate for a tiny degree in width so our visual field relies on scanning faces, moving our gaze typically from eye to eye, which is how the brain uses what it knows to fill in the gaps.

"Scanning is what an audience typically does, regardless of whether a close-up is in 2D or 3D," says Sieverts. "But the other problem for emotional perception of faces is caused by shadows and other environmental factors. These will strongly interfere with the comparison of left and right side scans in 2D because shadows are asymmetric 'noise.'"

Stereopsis, Sieverts infers, helps us to remove shading and other environmental "noise" from our perception of the surface shape. "Scanning and stereopsis together help us determine symmetry and thus the true emotional state of the person or character. If you are examining the person in this intimate situation in effect you are trying to read their mind or perhaps their soul."

Director Robert Zemeckis, stereoscopic supervisor Rob Engle and the editing team, experimented with the close-up on *Beowulf* (2007), which used performance capture and CGI to recount the ancient legend.

"We played with how much roundness we would apply to a face, going back to this idea that you connect more with a round face than a flat face," explains Engle. "We did an experiment with 'tuning' how much roundness we would put into a character, guided by the emotion of the scene.

"The main character of *Beowulf* is being constantly switched from a position of power— or at least he thinks he is in power—to a position of weakness where someone else has power over him. When he believes he is in power we gave him a fuller, rounded face and in positions of weakness or perceived weakness, we would flatten the face a little. It was subtle, but we wanted to experiment with this idea of using the dimension of the character's face to help support the story."

"When we look at a person in real life, no matter how close or far they are, you sense the roundness of their face," he adds. "And you sense their humanity. 3D brings you closer to the sense that that person is real. If it is round then your brain tells you it's real. If it's flat and muscles aren't moving right, then your brain says something is wrong."

For Letteri, whose most recent work includes Peter Jackson's 3D production of *The Hobbit*, there is a subtle dividing line when using 3D to heighten the drama of an intimate moment, and of killing that moment by overplaying the 3D.

He offers his perspective on how the Gollum/Smeagol monologue, performed by Andy Serkis in the original Rings trilogy, might have been shot in 3D. This is the key sequence where the two sides of the character's split personality come into conflict.

"What 3D would have brought to a scene like that is the feeling that you are physically in the space with Gollum, but you don't want to introduce anything that is going to distract from the drama, because the drama is really what that shot is about," says Letteri. "We probably would have kept it very simple and focused right on his face.

"There are a few moments when he becomes Gollum when he leans in kind of threateningly—those might be moments where you have him lean in front of the screen a little but only as a natural consequence of his body language."

Serkis comments that "You could have placed him physiologically in a different space... and played up his paranoia. I think that would have been an interesting thing to do."

When Scorsese began preparing *Hugo* he felt that "I was looking at moving statues. Faces in particular were given a special intimacy. 3D makes characters more accessible for the audience. If subtly done 3D allows the audience to become more immersed in the narrative and in an understanding of a character's behavior. I found this to be very

---

Andy Serkis, Actor and Second Unit Director, *The Hobbit*

Photo by Iva Lenard

Bringing his unique perspective as both an actor and director, Andy Serkis shares the idea that 3D should be used in support of story and character and not to overwhelm either.

"You don't want the audience to step out of the story at any time so you need to be very judicious about how to use 3D dramatically," he says. "The only reason you draw attention to a moment is if it is intensified, either emotionally or dramatically and is therefore a natural fit with the narrative. The rest of the time 3D is to be used sparingly and to bring you into a world."

In terms of blocking an actor's position in 3D space Serkis describes the technique as "like racking focus to a moment. But you are racking focus to a thought or a feeling."

Racking focus is the practice of shifting the focal point of an image from foreground to background, or vice versa.

Erik Aadahl, MPSE, Sound Designer, Supervising Sound Editor, *Monsters vs. Aliens*, *Transformers: Dark of the Moon*

Image courtesy Greg P. Russell.

"Sound can connect very, very powerfully with our brain and our bodies, and create profoundly emotional experiences such as fear and comfort," says Aadahl. "That is as true in 2D as it is in 3D but once you couple innovations like Dolby 7.1 Surround Sound, which allows you to use a more precise sound mix, with stereoscopic imagery, the overall effect helps the brain and eye to coordinate better psycho-acoustically."

Dolby 7.1 Surround Sound is gradually being introduced to cinemas worldwide and differs from current Dolby 5.1 Surround Sound by splitting the surround and rear channel effects into four channels, instead of combining them. This means that side sound effects and ambience are directed speakers to the left and right of an audience, and rear sound effects and ambience are directed to two rear channels placed behind an audience.

"With surround sound you can close your eyes and by hearing alone you can get a sense of the space you are in," says Aadahl. "You can hear texture, you can [hear] direction. We have always been able to do this with speakers in front of the screen. But in concert with 3D imagery we can do so much more with the sound."

Transformers: Dark of the Moon, which was Oscar nominated for sound mixing and sound editing, used a 7.1 mix. Its climax features a battle in downtown Chicago which Aadahl considers a prime example of surround sound working with 3D in action sequences.

"[Director] Michael Bay's intention was to put your nose right in the action. Visually, bullets are coming right at you and flying past you. Sonically, we would make the bullets whiz right past your head to simulate the feeling of being in the middle of combat.

"There's a tomahawk missile launched into the city. The sequence was mixed so that you can hear the missile in the distance and therefore behind you in the rear speakers. Then when it rips onto the screen, we had it rip past your head, from the right back speaker to the right side wall speaker to the right speaker on the front of the screen and into the center. The aim is to make you really feel the image of that tomahawk ripping past you. We used every chance we could get to create that sense of movement."

Even with the same picture edit of the same film the sound mix can be different from 2D to 3D version. While working on *Monster vs. Aliens*, Aadahl noticed that in 3D his eye was being drawn to a different point on the screen than when watching in 2D.

"In 3D your eye might go to something in the foreground, and because your eye is being drawn to it sonically you want to feature that a little bit more. For example, if objects or characters are in front of the screen plane I would make an adjustment to the soundtrack because sonically it made sense to match aurally the visual awareness you are making of an object. So the mix was changed based on our reaction to the stereo pictures."

Aadahl echoes filmmakers from other disciplines in suggesting that it is in the quieter, more character-driven moments where the picture and sound is at its most powerful.

"On the most basic level you want to create an experience where the viewer is pulled into the moment and experiences everything that the character is experiencing. The intimate moments are what storytelling is all about. It is why we go to movies—to connect."

strong, so much so that when we did the final 3D pass on the movie, a few weeks before release, I brought the characters in medium close-ups out even more from the screen."

HUGO

"If you've ever wondered where your dreams come from….This is where they are made," says a character in Brian Selznick's novel *The Invention of Hugo Cabaret*, referring to the magic of filmmaking, a line repeated in Martin Scorsese's feature adaptation *Hugo*.

Scorsese shares that sense of reverence and affection for cinema as a home of fantastical storytelling. He resurrects the trailblazing film work of French magician Georges Méliès, who is credited among other things with injecting some of the first narratives and use of visual effects into cinema, and pays tribute to the spirit of this endeavor by using the most modern "machinery of creativity"—3D.

Set in 1930s Paris, *Hugo* is the tale of an adventurous and orphaned boy who lives within the walls of a large train station. He keep the clocks in time at the station, using a maze of tunnels and ladders to move around without being seen and in the company of a young girl Isabelle, he sets out to unlock the mystery of an abandoned self-operating robot which, when wound up, appears to be able to write a message. It transpires that the key to the automaton is connected to the history of an enigmatic toy store owner.

Fig. 6.3 Martin Scorsese (with actor Ben Kingsley as Georges Méliès): "Every shot is rethinking narrative."

Images from the motion picture 'Hugo' reproduced by permission of GK Films, LLC.
Jaap Buitendijk. © 2011 GK Films, LLC. All Rights Reserved..

Like Méliès, Scorsese delights in playing with the new storytelling tools at his disposal, deliberately offering some shots of swords placed jarringly out of screen as if to poke fun at critics who condemn such pointy-stick 3D as gimmicky. In *Hugo* its use is in keeping with the playful but rudimentary visual effects first devised by Méliès.

He exhibits bravura 3D moments in which trains are sent hurtling toward the audience, or trademark Steadicam shots which follow Hugo into, through, up, and down the labyrinthine passages of the station.

More importantly he has latched onto 3D as a storytelling device because the train station itself, the vertiginous clock tower with Parisian vistas, and the clockwork cogs, wheels, and mechanics of Hugo's private universe are ideal for illustrating space and depth.

"We are accustomed to 2D and the use of long focal lengths which compress everything," Scorsese says. "With 3D every shot is rethinking cinema because you have to decide what to do with depth. It forces you to rethink narrative and how to tell a story with a picture."

According to producer Graham King another reason for using 3D was to help reveal the innermost thoughts of the characters. He says, "As moviegoers, we don't have the advantage of the literature, in which you can become aware of Hugo's inner thoughts and feelings. But here, we have his extraordinary face and his actions. I think that certain images—particularly in 3D—cover so much territory that the book resonates in them" [1].

A Cumulative Art Form

Planning the film in stereo from the start, Scorsese involved his entire team, including cinematographer Robert Richardson, ASC; editor Thelma Schoonmaker, A.C.E; production designer Dante Ferretti; and visual effects supervisor Rob Legato.

"It's hard to simply separate out 3D and state with certainty what it brings to a drama," says Legato, who also served as second unit director/cameraman. "You may as well ask what function color alone has on the impact of the drama or how you divorce selective focus depth of field, lighting, and production design from the storytelling. The point is that when used as an integral part of the filmmaking process 3D helps create a unique emotional response that, were you to see the same film in 2D, then the emotional content would be diminished."

He elaborates: "Cinema is such a cumulative and collaborative art form that you need all of the elements in front of you to make the correct creative choice for any one shot or scene. In making *Hugo* we approached 3D with an artistic sensibility. If 3D helped to sell the sense of place, which in turn sells the character's story then you have blended 3D into the same category as production design, costume design, camera movement, blocking, lens choices, lighting cues, and depth of field. 3D then becomes an interdependent and interwoven part of the cinematic art form."

What is particularly striking in *Hugo* is the effectiveness with which production design, visual effects, and cinematography have worked together to incorporate depth and space into the story as distinct narrative elements. Depth and space are used to give *Hugo* its very strong presence of place—a vast, teeming, period-set train station situated in a romanticized metropolis (built on sound stages at UK studios Pinewood Shepperton and Longcross, and in CGI), which King describes as a "blend of realism and a heightened, imagined world" and for which Richardson aimed "to evoke the romance of Paris in the 1930s and yet not divorce the present."

Hugo begins with a virtuoso VFX sequence in which the camera moves from a high level vista of Paris and plunges headlong at the speed of a train into the heart of the bustling Montparnasse station, winding up on a boy's eyes framed within the station clock face. The very start of the scene was originally envisioned without snow but when Legato previsualized it he intuitively felt that the addition of snow would "ease the audience into the magical mood of the story" in part because "we can all relate to snow as a realistic three-dimensional experience.

"We designed every shot to feature a foreground, middle, and background and in this instance the snow became the foreground even when the virtual camera is 1000 feet in the air," Legato says. "We were always asking how the 3D adds to or subtracts from our understanding of the shot."

He says: "When you are creating a sense of place, a key part is spatial awareness. When designing the 3D you need to think about how big the space is. How tall are the ceilings? How close are the characters to other human beings on screen? How claustrophobic would or should you feel? As a child, what would your altered perception of the adult world be and how would you then relate it the characters?"

Fig. 6.4 The filmmakers sought to create a sense of place by giving the audience spatial clues in production design (foreground, middle, and background) and cinematography as shown by this scene in the bookstore.

Images from the motion picture 'Hugo' reproduced by permission of GK Films, LLC.
Jaap Buitendijk. © 2011 GK Films, LLC. All Rights Reserved.

In one scene, the station inspector—a slightly pantomime villain played by Sasha Baron Cohen—catches and interrogates Hugo and Isabelle, who concocts a story to prevent her friend from being sent to an orphanage.

"The inspector is unsure whether to believe her story so to add to the suspense about whether they will get away with it, we framed a close-up shot of the inspector and then very slowly had him lean forward as if leering menacingly to Hugo and gradually dialed up the 3D. The audience begins to see the inspector from Hugo's perspective. We pushed and pushed the 3D in close-up on the inspector's face until it is looming larger than life and a little uncomfortably out of the screen. It's like when someone gets aggressive and gets a little too close to you, you feel threatened and invaded. The staging is very simple but the drama of the moment is heightened."

In a later scene, which echoes the classic Harold Lloyd sequence in *Safety Last*, Hugo escapes from the grasp of the inspector by climbing out onto a giant clock face, high above Paris. "The high angle shot, looking down so that you see a pair of feet dangling hundreds of meters above the traffic, is a familiar one but by adding a little bit of depth into the screen we could really emphasize the danger that Hugo is in," Legato says. "I just made a very simple camera move that shows the street and then shows the relationship with Hugo to the background. The sense of depth took it from being an ordinary shot to an extraordinary shot."

Another space that worked well in 3D was the bookstore, whose owner is played by Christopher Lee. According to Richardson: "When Hugo and Isabelle first walk in, there is a low three-shot—in which they are standing down below and Christopher Lee is perched up above. When we made this shot, Marty looked at me and said 'This shot would be impossible to accomplish in 2D.' To have a sense of the actual volume of a room is not possible in 2D. In 3D, with the angle we chose, you feel this room expand as if you were within it and you intuitively understood the relationship of objects in the room to each other in a way that is simply not possible in 2D."

For the scene in which Hugo and Isabelle venture to the library, location filming took place at the Bibliothèque Sainte-Geneviève. Richardson had prepared lighting cranes outside the windows to simulate sunshine, but when it was time to film, the sun came cascading into the voluminous library, one window at a time.

"Some atmosphere was added with a white smoke, so we could define the rays of light," describes stereographer Demetri Portelli. "On a 3D monitor, they looked like solid beams of platinum. In my experience this can only be achieved by shooting in 3D.

Filming native 3D [capturing 3D on set with a motorized rig] I can move each camera's lens around an object from two different positions, just like the eyes in our head 'see' from different angles. This process enables us to build objects with volume and gives the images in the film a wonderful physical tangibility" [2].

The air of the train station received similar treatment, to give viewers an impression of the age and feel of the place by adding layers of realism. This decision was made early in production when Richardson and Scorsese were viewing rushes.

"Bob and Marty noticed that there were floating dust particles in their (screening) tent and dust in the scene and that they couldn't tell them apart," recalls Legato. "Instead of deciding to remove or minimize the dust in post they decided to add even more."

During later scenes Scorsese had a member of the crew fan tiny bits of goose down into the shot to resemble dust "so that it invades the audience's space in a non-obvious way," observes Legato. "Dust seems like such a natural thing to ignore yet it adds a subtle layer helping you to understand the positioning of objects in the foreground, middle ground, and background."

Similarly, steam was added occasionally, and almost imperceptibly, emerging from screen plane to the edge of the frame.

"This again helped to stage the scene, and to give a sense that you are part of a story happening around you rather than just being played out in front of you," says Legato.

"Instead of a being an obvious, in your face visual effect we wanted the audience to experience a sensation of depth. You don't necessarily need to describe a scene in words if you can feel it and if you can feel it it's usually a much more powerful moment than anything else."

On any movie, a color palette is used to help create mood and atmosphere, for instance, of warmth or of being cold. With *Hugo*, Richardson explored the use of color to further enhance the feeling of depth that was being created with the 3D digital camera system (a combination of Arri cameras and Cameron|Pace Group rigs). An Oscar winner for *JFK* and *The Aviator*, Richardson won his third Oscar for *Hugo*, his first 3D film (and his first use of a digital camera).

"I found that a mix of cold temperatures and warmer temperatures could help define space, in addition to light and dark," he says. "It also helped greatly in defining how successful the 3D was, when we wanted 3D to be expanded or subtracted. We worked with a full blue tone and various levels of warmer tones in combination, which I had not done in other films to this extent, certainly not for the purposes of enhancing the sense of depth."

Richardson's choice of palette was influenced by his decision to emulate Autochromes, a photographic process patented by the Lumières at the turn of the 20th century, which used dyed potato starch on photosensitive glass plates to create full color transparencies.

Tungsten lights with a full blue gel (or tint) were hung overhead, while the stage was surrounded by tungsten sources so that they could derive either warmer or colder hues. "In essence this created a slight blue backlight that separates the layers of depth from the rest of scene," explains Legato, who had to match Richardson's choices when shooting the second unit. "The blue was shot at such a low exposure that the tone is really only picked up in the Autochrome emulation color correction process (in postproduction)."

Fig. 6.5 In making *Hugo*, Martin Scorsese says he discovered that faces are given a special intimacy with 3D.

Images from the motion picture 'Hugo' reproduced by permission of GK Films, LLC.
Jaap Buitendijk. © 2011 GK Films, LLC. All Rights Reserved.

Richardson previewed every shot prior to capture on a 3D monitor. "If at any point I felt the depth was not as desired I would ask Ian Kincaid (the gaffer) to add a particular color," explains Richardson. "That addition might begin with white or a slightly warm tone. The effect would be seen immediately and we responded to the impact of either light or color on a scene. Furthermore the sequences were designed to move with time, meaning morning, afternoon, night. The light reflected this framework but with artistic liberty. I would often add colors or subtract color to force the eye onto a particular plane."

Creativity Is Analog

Prior to filming, Scorsese had primed the crew by screening several movies that inspired him. These included David Lean's *Great Expectations* (1946), which is told from a young boy's perspective as well as 3D classics from the 1950s, including Hitchcock's suspense thriller *Dial M for Murder*, musical *Kiss Me Kate*, and horror film *House of Wax*.

"Marty explained that these films illustrated the nature of the 3D that he wanted to go back to," Richardson says. "He wanted to push away from the idea of using very subtle 3D and encouraged us to be unafraid of playing with depth. He wanted to have more variables, a wider palette of 3D that would range from a subtle 3D up to more extreme levels, just to see what worked for what scene."

For all its strength as a narrative element Scorsese's use of 3D in *Hugo* reveals the extent to which the medium lies unexplored. In *Hugo,* Scorsese delights in pushing back against the perceived boundaries of its use.

When he announced the film was to be made in 3D, Scorsese says he was inundated with advice, almost all of which was bad.

"I was explained the rules. I'm not sure if I understood them but I pushed against the perceived boundaries with a project that seemed to lend itself naturally to 3D. You learn that there are limits when it becomes painful to the eyes, but you keep on testing and if it couldn't be done, we'd have seen it on the set, on the monitor."

For all the warnings about keeping 3D within certain ranges, Scorsese showed that risks can and should be taken.

"Creative decision making is an analog process, as opposed to a digital one, which people need to see and feel in order to make an artistic judgment," believes Legato. "Exacting and specific technical instructions mean nothing in itself except as a translation of artistic direction. Consequently Marty would talk about 3D on set more in terms of

'I'm not feeling the depth' or 'I want more' or 'that's too much,' which is more or less the language of stage direction, in essence the way a director would give feedback to actors.

"On a Martin Scorsese film everything—from 3D to lighting—is set up to not interfere with the analog filmmaking process. When the digital mechanics are removed from every part of the film, what is left is a concentration on the picture, which we'd look at and discuss as if it were a painting or a sculpture—'Is it too light or too dark or do we need more depth or detail and does the emotion come through?'

"Since everybody had a chance to see all of Marty's cinematic influences in preproduction on the big screen, we all subconsciously understood what we were trying to achieve so that when a decision arose everybody was instinctively on the same page.

"A director needs to see 3D, feel it, master and embrace it live and on set in order for them to stamp their personality on it," urges Legato. "It's about using 3D as part of the whole set of tools that will now take filmmakers to the next level of movie making."

Fig. 6.6 3D was exaggerated in places to enhance surrealism and for comic effect.

Filmed four times previously, notably in 1949 and 1974, F Scott Fitzgerald's *The Great Gatsby* is retold by director Baz Luhrmann as a parable for our times. It charts the lives and loves of an elite and the impact on them of sudden wealth.

We follow would-be writer Nick Carraway as he leaves the Midwest and comes to New York in the spring of 1922, an era of loosening morals, glittering jazz, and prohibition. Carraway lands next door to a mysterious, party-giving millionaire, Jay Gatsby, and across the bay from his cousin, Daisy, and her philandering husband, Tom Buchanan. Nick is drawn into the captivating world of the super rich, and their illusions, loves, and deceits.

Whereas an expected visual treatment of the period might feature scenically aged sets, static cameras, and classic lighting, Luhrmann had a wider ambition. The film is crafted with carefully framed wide shots in the manner of movie classics from the 1930s and '40s, but he has also set out to create a sense of reality and modernity, to give a sense of being present in the Jazz Age where everything was new, technologically advanced, and sophisticated.

Luhrmann explains: "I grew mindful that Fitzgerald himself was obsessed with all things new and modern, especially as he was writing Gatsby: the new cinema, the new radio, the new skyscraper, this new thing called jazz, the automobile. In the end, I felt that I couldn't address his Gatsby as a much-loved museum piece. My mindset was to address it something like Fitzgerald might have, as a piece in an age full of new possibilities enabled by new ideas and new technologies. Seen this way, shooting in 3D made perfect sense."

The color and the textures of the production design are vibrant, and enhanced by the use of digital film technology (Red Epic cameras and 3Ality Technica systems, marshaled by Jeff Amaral) and the newest cinematic storytelling format, 3D.

Dial M for Preparation

Although originated as a 3D project, Luhrmann conducted a series of tests to help him grasp the visual grammar that would work for the story. These included a spell in Los Angeles at the Sony 3D Technology Center and time at Bazmark's New York offices with key cast including Leonardo Di Caprio and Tobey Maguire in the autumn of 2010.

In these lab-style tests, using a rig similar to the one used in final production, Luhrmann was able to demonstrate to himself how a performance might be captured using stereo cameras. He later used a 3D camcorder to help scout locations while production designer and co-producer Catherine Martin used a handheld 3D camera to envision how her costume designs would look.

From *Strictly Ballroom* through *Romeo + Juliet, Moulin Rouge*, and *Australia*, Luhrmann's films have been characterized by a flamboyant visual style and choreographed flows of movement within scenes. The use of stereo as a medium distinct from, but drawing on, the theater stage would seem to fit naturally into this sensibility.

Having adapted breakthrough film *Strictly Ballroom* from his own play while studying at Sydney's National Institute of Dramatic Art, the director appreciated the similarities that the 3D format has to a theatrical stage performance, where he could create depth by blocking actors and designing set pieces.

"Like most people, I initially viewed 3D used as a sort of flashy visual effect," says Luhrmann. "That changed as Jim Cameron was developing *Avatar*, and I saw him do a lecture on 3D, and became really fascinated. Generously, he took the time to take CM [Catherine Martin] and I through the early development of that film, as well as letting us see some of the deep-sea 3D explorations he had done. Both opened my eyes (along with everyone else's I think) to the enormous possibilities of the medium, a potential which was cemented the moment I saw Hitchcock's *Dial M for Murder*.

"That film proved, for me, how fundamentally different 3D is in terms of dramatic staging; it has a force that is born quite simply from its ability to capture great actors 'acting,' playing against each other in a tight space and toward the camera, something like the theater."

Warner Bros, which owned the rights to this renowned stereoscopic film, helped organize screenings of the 1982 restored 3D print. "When Baz told me he wanted to shoot his adaptation of the story in 3D I looked at him askance," relates Executive Producer Barrie M. Osborne. "I was initially skeptical. Baz arranged for me to see *Dial M for Murder* in a screening, which required two projectors and a reel change. I expected to stay for just one reel but ended up so engrossed I watched it all."

Osborne's research also took in *PINA* and Herzog's *Cave of Forgotten Dreams* but it was the drama of *Dial M for Murder* that convinced him that 3D was right for Gatsby.

"You experience the interactions of other actors in a scene. Instead of cutting in coverage Hitchcock created more dramatic impact simply by holding on the shot," he says. "The 3D heightened the dramatic tension that you felt for the characters and the situation. I understood why Baz wanted to use 3D for *The Great Gatsby* and suggested we screen it as part of full cast rehearsal in New York."

The scene in which Grace Kelly's character stretches agonizingly for a pair of scissors placed prominently within the audience's reach as she attempts to defend herself is the most quoted, but it was the mise-en-scene of the film from which Luhrmann drew the most inspiration.

Dial M for Murder was itself an adaptation of a successful stage play that takes place in the confines of a single setting, the living room of a London flat. Although Hitchcock broadened this to include scenes in a gentleman's club and some external street views, the majority of the drama occurs in one place and with a handful of actors.

"The most important aspects are the characters and the dialogue between two or three people, mostly in a single [living] room," describes stereographer Alonso Homs. "Hitchcock's skill in using stereo has helped put the audience into that cramped space, at times playing on the claustrophobia as we feel the tension of characters unsure if one of them is the murderer. At the same time the stereo and the set design has made the characters emotionally more accessible because we are better able to read their motivation."

This was the single biggest takeaway for Luhrmann's team; that 3D could be used to enhance performance and draw out the humanity in a character. It became the overriding goal for the stereo approach to *The Great Gatsby*. "The main dramatic tension in the story is between Gatsby, Buchanan, and Daisy," says Osborne. "In 3D you feel the force of these characters and the power of the actor's personality comes across on screen so much more."

Luhrmann himself says, "As I approached *Gatsby* I had the idea already in my head that the big special effect finale for us would not be what we might do that is visually rich in 3D, but what a one-of-a-kind ensemble of actors might do in a single room in the Plaza Hotel, tearing at each others' hearts and feelings during a ten-page scene."

Gatsby's Stereo Design

Luhrmann, Homs, and director of photography Simon Duggan, ACS (Australian Cinematographers Society) wanted to provide a realism to their characters so that the actor's performance, much of which was internalized, would be better perceived by the audience. In turn this meant understanding where to put the camera and what to put around the character to deliver an appropriate sense of volume and depth. "Very broadly: our approach is that if a character is volumetric it makes them more human," Homs says.

For Lead 3D Engineer Jeff Amaral, the approach was bold: "3D gives so much more information to the viewer and asks them to look around a scene so that the story hangs on the strength of the performances and the staging."

Attention turned to translating this idea into a practical shooting style. For Homs, that meant understanding the spatial flow of the entire piece without being overly prescriptive, aside from a few previsualized scenes where visual effects played heavily.

"It was important to find the right range [and] amount of depth and volume that would work for this story," says Homs, who relates stereo design to lighting design. "Just as you wouldn't have a single scene in a serious drama that is lit in film noir style and immediately following another keyed for comedy, so you shouldn't chop and change 3D styles within a picture or overemphasize its presence," he says.

He observes that director Sidney Lumet planned to film *Network* as gritty and more realistic in the beginning and how the look would slowly progress through the film to gradually resemble the fake reality of a car commercial.

"There is never one scene from another in which you sit up and notice the transition, it's just a very elegant progression," says Homs. "I'm not saying that works for every movie in terms of having an arc of depth that mirrors the narrative—you can move up and down according to the story—but the point is that it is only worth bringing attention to the 3D element if it helps the story. While *The Great Gatsby* makes considerable use of negative parallax we intend to keep an audience tuned to the story world, not pull them out of it. There should always be motivation behind it, a thought-out approach."

He elaborates: "By subtle use of negative parallax we can allow a character to feel excluded from the world that they are in and by implication closer, literally, to the character and closer emotionally to the performance. The technique allows us to find that connection between audience and character."

Having workshopped a number of scenes, Luhrmann had developed an approach to 3D that carefully considered lensing and camera movement, and had an awareness of creating physical depth cues for shooting interior and exterior locations.

"We went in with a very flexible approach to the choreography of the camera movement and the actor's blocking," says Duggan. "Although there were obvious moments in the script which called for maximum volume and/or negative parallax the stereo depth was often adjusted as the scene blocking developed and opportunities arose."

Catherine Martin, Producer, Production Designer, Costume Designer, *The Great Gatsby* (also Producer, Production Designer *Australia, Moulin Rouge!, Romeo + Juliet*)

Image courtesy Bazmark Films.

"Comparing my past work with Baz on all of his films and our current work in 3D, it has become apparent to me that Baz has always tried to create the effect of three dimensions in all of his two-dimensional films. He has done so through careful framing, ensuring there is a sense of action in the background, middle ground, and foreground, and by creating a sense of texture and opulence through quick cutting—all fuelled by a desire to fully immerse the audience in the world he is creating.

"My experience of working in the three-dimensional medium has been one of great surprise. Most surprising is that as well as being on the cutting edge of technical cinematography, 3D has allowed Baz to discover a renewed profoundness in the actor's craft. Just watching great acting in a 3D close-up is a revelation without any other bells and whistles.

"Baz's love of texture and his great attention to detail demands the design of his films to be rich with storytelling material so when it came to designing a movie in 3D, I realized that most of the design tools I had used in the past could be used to great effect. Baz also asked me to focus on structural cues within the scenery such as arches, pillars, and objects that repeat back into the space in order to give the audience eye cues that allow them to read depth and observe the action in different planes simultaneously."

Bringing the Close-up Closer

In the desire to convey realism, the filmmakers put great effort into understanding what would be the best use of volume in any shot, with particular emphasis on an actor's face. During location shooting in and around Sydney (winter 2011), the production team explained that this meant confronting some of the conventions of filmmaking; the over the shoulder shot for two-person dialogue and the close-up.

"Drama has the most classical film language of any genre, which is why shooting drama in 3D is a challenge," says Homs. "The close-up is the essence of what the filmmaker is trying to achieve in a drama, which is to get to the emotion of that moment and that character.

"A typical close-up will be shot with a long lens and an object, perhaps a person's shoulder, will be blurred in the foreground to give an illusion of depth. The foreground object places the person in the space and the amount of blur tells you how close you are to it. In 3D this is unnecessary and uncomfortable and defeats the purpose of putting the viewer in the space with the characters because this is not the way we see in real life.

"We never look at another person's face with something else an inch from our eyeball. The use of long focal lengths tends to compress the space and flatten out the human face and goes against the virtues of 3D. With a willingness to shoot close-ups on wide 32mm and 40mm lenses, getting rid of the blurred foreground for these shots and being conscious that the closest object to the lens will have the most volume, you will capture volume and depth."

According to Duggan, "In 3D there is nothing like being right in the face of the actor or close up on a detail with a wide lens. It probably felt slightly invasive at the start but once our actors saw the results, they loved it. A close-up with 3D volume and detail is incredible as it heightens the viewer's access to the actor's emotions. You can read the subtlest of expression and look straight into their eyes."

Although the mirror boxes on the production's 3Ality rigs are small, lighting the actor's faces in close-up to avoid shadows was a challenge. To solve this, Duggan created a special eye-light with an LED strip that lined the perimeter of the front of the mirror box.

"For extreme close-ups Baz was interested in getting the lighting to reflect the mood or situation of the actor, so while this was as unobtrusive as possible we would be in close to the actor, much like lighting a commercial pack shot," explains Duggan. "I feel that the way the human brain processes and fuses the stereo images together is the first part of convincing the viewer that the images are real. We wanted to maintain this sense of reality using lenses similar to the human field of view (with 16mm the widest and rarely going longer than 65mm), and to use a natural depth of field to give a more immersive experience than possible in 2D."

Duggan, Homs, and Luhrmann soon found that the medium shot, capturing more volume of an actor's body in a more realistic way, meant that they didn't necessarily require a conventional close-up.

One scene shows Gatsby at home, sitting down and talking on the telephone. The script called for a close-up of the ring on his finger.

"When it came to shooting the scene Baz and Simon selected a medium shot and Gatsby just happened to have his hand on the armrest of the couch so that his ring finger was positioned slightly closer to camera than anything else," explains Homs. "When we watched this back we found ourselves scanning through the frame to read Gatsby's emotions but as we did so our eyes were also alighting on the ring. The scene is not necessarily about the ring and wouldn't stand out in 2D but in 3D the audience's attention is brought to it in a subtle manner with no close-up of the ring needed. It was a perfect balance between reading the character's feelings and pointing out an object that was important to the story without having to shoot a close-up."

In another example, Tom Buchanan joins Gatsby at his mansion for a party. They are sitting together when Gatsby's butler comes in to tell him that someone is on the phone.

"As the butler comes close to Gatsby's ear and gives him the message there is a perfect layering of Tom and Jay and the butler so that you can easily read the emotion passing across their faces," says Homs. "It feels like three close-ups in one.

"The physicality of the performance is much more readable. You don't need to go as close to the face, and you don't necessarily need to go to the eyes but when you do close up on the eyes in 3D it makes that shot all the more powerful. You are then looking at a face that has volume, where there is more information to scan and more emotion to read."

Extreme close-ups were selected for intense moments, while mid-shots with two or three characters in frame at varying distances from the lens conveyed not only "the interaction between the characters in frame but additional detail and volume so that the viewer can find their own close-up on any character within the frame," says Duggan. "An actor's body language is amplified in 3D. The shot is easier to read because you are a lot more aware of detail."

A key moment in the story is the revelation that Daisy receives when she sees Gatsby for the first time since he had gone to war. In the interim time Daisy decides to marry Tom Buchanan instead of her true love so she is surprised by the reunion arranged by Gatsby, in collusion with Nick Carraway, on his return.

As Daisy enters Carraway's cottage she waits surrounded by bouquets of flowers. The flowers fill the foreground and then as the camera closes in we move to Daisy's face. She feels something is not quite right.

She catches sight of herself in a mirror and at this moment the stereo is a flat 2D reflection of herself, as if to reflect the person she had become while estranged from

Gatsby. The person she has become is not fully formed, but shallow. Something of her is missing.

According to Homs this was not planned but something that happened on the day when blocking the scene. The camera then pans down the hallway, the stereo fully rounded and full of depth now as if to reveal an abundance of life that would have been hers had she stayed and married Gatsby.

A little later in the same sequence, Duggan has used a 20mm lens to frame Daisy, Gatsby, and Carraway in a three-shot in the bungalow's living room. The camera is closest to Gatsby, who is in profile with Carraway and Daisy in the background sitting on a couch at the same distance to the camera as each other. Gatsby's head pokes a little into negative space as if to suggest that the audience follow his intimate thoughts at that moment.

"A lot of that scene's drama is played out in silence," says Homs. "We attempt to close the distance between viewer and character just by using wider lenses and negative parallax to make the emotion of the moment more intimate. If the most important element of a movie is the story and the thing that tells that story is character then why would you not want to involve something that makes characters more accessible?"

Depth in Production Design

There are common techniques in 2D filmmaking to direct the viewer to an actor or point of interest, or to create depth by using devices such as a shallow depth of field, soft focus foreground objects, long lenses, and backlighting that verges on silhouette. These are often less effective in 3D as they go contrary to the effect of creating a convincing realistic world for the viewer, according to Duggan.

Instead Duggan's approach to lighting *Gatsby* was to accent the volume of the stereo image by maintaining a certain amount of roundness to the lighting and to show detail by adding layers from foreground to background.

"I found that a backlit foreground image against a dark background looks like a cardboard cutout," he says. "In most cases Baz had freedom to move the camera anywhere he wanted. Many times we would start with a wide shot such as a party scene and end up on a close-up, often employing handheld lighting starting outside of the wide shot frame with the gaffer running in behind the camera and landing on the close-up. We also had all of our lighting running through dimmer boards so at any time we could cross-fade the lighting as the camera moved around the scene."

Continues Duggan, "The camera is constantly on the move throughout the film, placed on telescoping cranes, dollies, and Steadicam. Depth perception is increased within each scene by having the camera travel through architectural features such as arches and doorways or exterior foliage. The weather and seasonal changes play an important part of the storytelling with snow, rain, blowing leaves, and smoke additionally used to enhance dimensionality. The camera even passes through tunnels of people to create a continuous reveal of characters and the spaces they inhabit."

The latter is a part of a scene in which Nick enters Gatsby's mansion for the first time. A party is in full swing and the excess of the period is on display, illustrated by a richness of texture and color in set and costume. There's a flurry of movement as Nick enters the main hallway, tracked on Steadicam and from his point of view.

Fast movement of objects across the camera in stereo can cause a disconcerting strobing effect. To get around this and to still use a lot of foreground crosses in the party scenes,

Fig. 6.7 Baz Luhrmann on the set of *The Great Gatsby*: "Shooting in 3D made perfect sense."
Image courtesy Bazmark Films.

Luhrmann choreographed actors to move either on a diagonal line towards and past or away from the lens.

"The 3D means we are better able to read the world around those characters—so being able to read the texture on the walls, the furniture or feather hats at a party, water in a pool, the costumes, and so on helps you understand the character's motivation better," says Homs. "It helps you understand who they are and what they are going through and helps to bring you into their world."

Author's Note:

At the 84th Academy Awards, Hugo *was nominated for 11 Oscars and won five, including cinematography, visual effects, art direction, sound editing and sound mixing.*

REFERENCES

[1-2] Hugo Production Notes © MMXI Paramount Pictures Corporation. All rights reserved.

Index

Note: Page numbers with "f" denote figures; "b" boxes.